Mastering
Internet of Things
Concepts, Techniques, and Applications

Nikhilesh Mishra,
Author

Website
https://www.nikhileshmishra.com

Copyright Information

Dedication

This book is lovingly dedicated to the cherished memory of my father, **Late Krishna Gopal Mishra**, and my mother**, Mrs. Vijay Kanti Mishra.** Their unwavering support, guidance, and love continue to inspire me.

Table of Contents

Author's Preface

Welcome to the captivating world of the knowledge we are about to explore! Within these pages, we invite you to embark on a journey that delves into the frontiers of information and understanding.

Charting the Path to Knowledge

Dive deep into the subjects we are about to explore as we unravel the intricate threads of innovation, creativity, and problem-solving. Whether you're a curious enthusiast, a seasoned professional, or an eager learner, this book serves as your gateway to gaining a deeper understanding.

Your Guiding Light

From the foundational principles of our chosen field to the advanced frontiers of its applications, we've meticulously crafted this book to be your trusted companion. Each chapter is an expedition, guided by expertise and filled with practical insights to empower you on your quest for knowledge.

What Awaits You

- **Illuminate the Origins:** Embark on a journey through the historical evolution of our chosen field, discovering key milestones that have paved the way for breakthroughs.

- **Demystify Complex Concepts:** Grasp the fundamental principles, navigate intricate concepts, and explore practical applications.

- **Mastery of the Craft:** Equip yourself with the skills and knowledge needed to excel in our chosen domain.

Your Journey Begins Here

As we embark on this enlightening journey together, remember that mastery is not just about knowledge but also the wisdom to apply it. Let each chapter be a stepping stone towards unlocking your potential, and let this book be your guide to becoming a true connoisseur of our chosen field.

So, turn the page, delve into the chapters, and immerse yourself in the world of knowledge. Let curiosity be your compass, and let the pursuit of understanding be your guide.

Begin your expedition now. Your quest for mastery awaits!

Sincerely,

Nikhilesh Mishra,

Author

CHAPTER 1

Introduction to IoT

The Internet of Things (IoT) is a technological revolution that has reshaped the way we interact with the world around us. It represents the convergence of the physical and digital realms, where everyday objects and devices are connected to the internet, enabling them to collect, exchange, and analyze data like never before. This transformative concept has the potential to touch every aspect of our lives, from the way we live and work to how we manage resources and make decisions.

In this introductory chapter, we will embark on a journey through the fascinating world of IoT, exploring its origins, key concepts, and the profound impact it has on industries, businesses, and individuals alike. We will delve into the core principles that underpin IoT, shedding light on the intricate web of sensors, connectivity, and data that powers this phenomenon. Additionally, we will navigate through the benefits that IoT offers, as well as the challenges it poses, setting the stage for a comprehensive exploration of this dynamic field throughout the book. Whether you are a seasoned professional or a curious newcomer, this chapter will lay the foundation for your understanding of IoT and

1

set the context for the deep dive that lies ahead. Welcome to the exciting realm of the Internet of Things.

A. Definition and Evolution of IoT

The Internet of Things (IoT) is a transformative concept that has ushered in a new era of connectivity, data exchange, and automation. At its core, IoT refers to a network of physical objects or "things" embedded with sensors, software, and connectivity, allowing them to collect and exchange data with other devices and systems over the internet. This interconnectedness empowers these objects to make intelligent decisions and perform actions without the need for direct human intervention.

Evolution of IoT: From Concept to Reality

The roots of IoT can be traced back to the early 20th century when inventors and futurists envisioned a world where machines could communicate and collaborate seamlessly. However, it wasn't until the late 20th century that significant advancements in technology and the proliferation of the internet set the stage for the IoT's emergence.

1. **Milestones in IoT Evolution**:

    - **1990s:** The concept of IoT began to take shape with the development of RFID (Radio-Frequency

Identification) technology, which allowed objects to be tracked and identified remotely.

- **2000s:** The convergence of technologies such as RFID, wireless communication, and the growing prevalence of the internet laid the groundwork for the IoT. Initially, it found applications in supply chain management and logistics.

- **2010s:** The IoT gained momentum as miniaturized sensors, low-power processors, and wireless connectivity became more affordable and accessible. This period witnessed the rapid expansion of IoT into various industries, including smart homes, healthcare, agriculture, and industrial automation.

- **Present:** IoT has become an integral part of modern life. Smartphones, wearable devices, and smart home appliances are commonplace, while industries are leveraging IoT for predictive maintenance, remote monitoring, and data-driven decision-making.

2. **Key Concepts**:

- **Sensors:** IoT devices rely on sensors to collect data from their environment. These sensors can measure everything from temperature and humidity to motion and light.

- **Connectivity:** IoT devices use various communication protocols, including Wi-Fi, Bluetooth, cellular networks, and low-power options like LoRa and NB-IoT, to transmit data to central servers or other devices.

- **Data Processing:** Collected data is processed either at the edge (on the device itself) or in the cloud, depending on the application's requirements.

- **Automation:** IoT devices can trigger actions based on the data they collect. For instance, a smart thermostat can adjust the temperature in a room based on occupancy and temperature readings.

- **Scalability:** IoT networks can range from small-scale deployments in homes to vast industrial networks with thousands of devices, showcasing the scalability of the concept.

- **Interoperability:** Interoperability standards and protocols ensure that IoT devices from different manufacturers can work together seamlessly.

The Impact of IoT on Society and Industry:

IoT's evolution has had a profound impact on various aspects of society and industry:

1. **Efficiency and Productivity:** In the industrial sector, IoT has

enabled predictive maintenance, optimizing machine uptime and reducing downtime costs.

2. **Healthcare:** Wearable IoT devices and remote patient monitoring systems have transformed healthcare, allowing for real-time health data tracking and early intervention.

3. **Smart Cities:** IoT is driving the development of smart city solutions, including intelligent traffic management, waste disposal, and energy-efficient infrastructure.

4. **Consumer Convenience:** Smart homes equipped with IoT devices provide convenience and energy savings through automated lighting, heating, and security systems.

5. **Environmental Sustainability:** IoT is used in environmental monitoring to track air quality, water quality, and climate data, contributing to sustainability efforts.

6. **Data Insights:** The massive volumes of data generated by IoT devices provide valuable insights for decision-makers in various fields, from business to public policy.

In conclusion, the definition and evolution of IoT reflect a remarkable journey from a conceptual idea to a tangible reality that is reshaping how we live and work. This interconnected network of objects, empowered by sensors, connectivity, and data processing, has the potential to drive innovation across industries and improve the quality of life for individuals worldwide. As we delve deeper into the intricacies of IoT in the subsequent chapters, we will uncover the myriad opportunities and challenges that lie ahead in this exciting technological landscape.

B. Key Concepts (Sensors, Connectivity, Data) in IoT

In the realm of the Internet of Things (IoT), three fundamental concepts form the cornerstone of its functionality and transformative power: Sensors, Connectivity, and Data. Understanding these concepts is crucial to grasping the intricacies of how IoT works and its far-reaching impact across industries and daily life.

1. Sensors: The Eyes and Ears of IoT

Sensors are the sensory organs of the IoT ecosystem. They serve as the bridge between the physical and digital worlds, enabling IoT devices to perceive and gather data from the environment. These data points can be as diverse as temperature, humidity, light, motion, pressure, and even more specialized measurements in specific applications.

Types of Sensors in IoT:

- **Environmental Sensors:** These sensors monitor parameters like temperature, humidity, air quality, and atmospheric pressure. They are essential in applications like weather monitoring, indoor climate control, and environmental conservation.

- **Motion and Proximity Sensors:** These sensors detect movement and the presence of objects within a defined range. They are widely used in security systems, smart lighting, and robotics.

- **Biometric Sensors:** Found in wearable devices, these sensors measure physiological data such as heart rate, blood pressure, and skin conductivity, enabling health and fitness tracking.

- **Image and Video Sensors:** Cameras and imaging sensors capture visual information, essential for surveillance, autonomous vehicles, and facial recognition systems.

- **Position and Location Sensors:** GPS and RFID are examples of sensors that provide precise location data, supporting navigation, logistics, and asset tracking.

2. Connectivity: The Digital Nervous System

Connectivity is the backbone of IoT, serving as the digital nervous system that enables IoT devices to communicate and share data. IoT devices use various communication protocols and technologies to transmit data to centralized servers, other devices, or the cloud.

Key Connectivity Technologies in IoT:

- **Wi-Fi:** Provides high-speed internet connectivity suitable for IoT devices in proximity to Wi-Fi access points. Common in smart homes and offices.

- **Bluetooth:** Ideal for short-range connections between IoT devices, often used in wearables and smart home applications.

- **Cellular Networks:** IoT devices equipped with SIM cards can connect to 2G, 3G, 4G, and 5G networks, enabling remote monitoring and control.

- **Low-Power Wide Area Networks (LPWAN):** Technologies like LoRa and Sigfox offer long-range, low-power connectivity for IoT devices in applications like agriculture and smart cities.

- **Mesh Networks:** IoT devices can form self-healing mesh networks, where each device acts as a node, relaying data to extend the network's reach and reliability.

3. Data: The Lifeblood of IoT

Data is at the heart of IoT's transformative potential. IoT devices generate vast amounts of data, and this data holds valuable insights that drive decision-making, automation, and efficiency improvements across various domains.

Data Aspects in IoT:

- **Data Collection:** IoT devices continuously collect data from their environment through sensors. This data can be structured (e.g., sensor readings) or unstructured (e.g., images or videos).

- **Data Processing:** Depending on the application, data processing can occur either at the device itself (edge computing) or in the cloud. Processing involves filtering, aggregation, and analysis to extract actionable insights.

- **Data Storage:** IoT data can be stored in various locations, including cloud servers, edge devices, and local databases. The choice depends on factors like data volume, latency requirements, and security considerations.

- **Data Security:** Protecting IoT data is paramount. Encryption, access control, and secure communication protocols are essential to safeguard sensitive information.

- **Data Analytics:** IoT data is a goldmine for analytics. Machine learning and artificial intelligence algorithms can uncover patterns, anomalies, and trends that inform decision-making.

The Synergy of Sensors, Connectivity, and Data:

The power of IoT lies in the synergy among these key concepts. Sensors capture real-world data, connectivity facilitates data transmission, and data, once processed and analyzed, fuels informed actions. This cycle of data-driven decision-making and automation drives efficiencies, enhances user experiences, and transforms industries ranging from healthcare and agriculture to manufacturing and smart cities.

In essence, IoT's ability to harness the physical world's data and integrate it into digital systems represents a paradigm shift with profound implications for society and businesses. As we explore deeper into IoT's various facets in subsequent chapters, we'll witness how these key concepts come together to create innovative solutions and address complex challenges.

C. IoT Ecosystem: Unveiling the Complexity of Connectivity

The Internet of Things (IoT) is more than just a collection of smart devices; it's a vast and intricate ecosystem that encompasses a multitude of components, players, and technologies working in concert to enable seamless connectivity and data exchange. Understanding the IoT ecosystem is crucial to appreciating the complexity and potential of this transformative technology landscape.

1. Core Elements of the IoT Ecosystem

a. IoT Devices: These are the physical "things" that form the foundation of IoT. These devices are embedded with sensors, actuators, and communication modules that enable them to collect data, process information, and interact with other devices or systems. IoT devices can range from simple sensors to complex machinery and can be found in various domains, including consumer electronics, industrial equipment, healthcare devices, and more.

b. Connectivity: At the heart of IoT is the network that enables devices to communicate. Connectivity options can vary widely depending on the use case. This includes wired connections (e.g., Ethernet), wireless technologies (e.g., Wi-Fi, cellular networks), and low-power, long-range options (e.g., LoRa, NB-IoT). The choice of connectivity impacts factors such as data transmission speed, range, and power consumption.

c. Data Processing and Analytics: IoT devices generate vast amounts of data. To make this data valuable, it needs to be processed, analyzed, and turned into actionable insights. This can occur at various levels, including on the device itself (edge computing), at a local gateway, or in the cloud. Data processing techniques range from basic filtering to advanced machine learning algorithms.

d. Cloud Infrastructure: The cloud serves as a central hub for storing and managing IoT data. Cloud platforms provide scalability, accessibility, and robust data storage and processing capabilities. They are often used for long-term data storage, data analytics, and remote device management.

e. IoT Applications: These are the software solutions and applications that leverage IoT data to provide value to end-users and organizations. IoT applications can be diverse, including smart home automation, industrial automation, healthcare monitoring, agriculture management, and more. These applications can run on various devices, including smartphones, tablets, and web interfaces.

f. Security Frameworks: Security is a paramount concern in the IoT ecosystem. Security frameworks and protocols are essential to protect IoT devices, data, and communication. This includes encryption, secure boot processes, authentication, access control, and regular security updates.

2. Key Players in the IoT Ecosystem

The IoT ecosystem involves a wide array of stakeholders, each contributing to its growth and development:

a. Device Manufacturers: These companies design and manufacture IoT devices, from simple sensors to complex machinery. They play a crucial role in shaping the capabilities and features of IoT hardware.

b. Connectivity Providers: Telecom companies and network providers offer the connectivity infrastructure that allows IoT devices to transmit data. They enable the IoT ecosystem to function by providing the necessary communication channels.

c. Cloud Service Providers: Companies like Amazon Web Services (AWS), Microsoft Azure, and Google Cloud provide cloud infrastructure and services for data storage, processing, and analytics. They offer scalable solutions for handling the massive volumes of data generated by IoT devices.

d. IoT Platform Providers: These companies offer specialized IoT platforms that streamline device management, data collection, and application development. These platforms often include tools for device provisioning, data visualization, and analytics.

e. Application Developers: Developers and software engineers create IoT applications and solutions tailored to specific use cases. They build the interfaces and algorithms that make IoT data useful and actionable.

f. Regulatory Bodies: Government agencies and industry associations establish regulations, standards, and certifications to ensure the security and interoperability of IoT devices and systems.

3. Complexity and Challenges

While the IoT ecosystem offers immense potential, it also

presents significant challenges. These include:

- **Interoperability:** Ensuring that devices from different manufacturers can communicate and work together seamlessly is a persistent challenge in IoT.

- **Security:** Protecting IoT devices and data from cyber threats and ensuring data privacy is an ongoing concern.

- **Scalability:** As the number of IoT devices continues to grow exponentially, scaling infrastructure and managing data become increasingly complex.

- **Data Management:** Dealing with the sheer volume and variety of IoT data requires robust data management and analytics solutions.

In conclusion, the IoT ecosystem is a dynamic and multifaceted network of devices, technologies, and stakeholders. Its complexity mirrors its potential, offering the promise of automation, efficiency, and innovation across industries. Understanding the various components and players in this ecosystem is essential for harnessing the full potential of IoT and addressing its challenges effectively.

D. Benefits and Challenges of the Internet of Things (IoT)

The Internet of Things (IoT) has ushered in a new era of connectivity and data-driven decision-making. While it offers numerous benefits, it also presents unique challenges that must be carefully navigated. In this exploration, we delve into both the advantages and complexities that define the IoT landscape.

Benefits of IoT:

1. **Efficiency and Automation:**

   - *Industrial Optimization:* In manufacturing and industrial settings, IoT enables predictive maintenance, reducing downtime and optimizing production processes.

   - *Supply Chain Enhancement:* IoT devices provide real-time tracking of goods, improving logistics, reducing spoilage, and enhancing overall supply chain efficiency.

   - *Smart Agriculture:* Farmers can optimize irrigation, monitor soil conditions, and automate crop management, leading to higher yields and reduced resource consumption.

2. **Data-Driven Insights:**

- *Business Intelligence:* IoT generates vast amounts of data, allowing organizations to make data-driven decisions, optimize operations, and enhance customer experiences.

- *Healthcare Advancements:* Remote patient monitoring and wearable devices offer real-time health data, improving patient care and allowing early intervention.

3. **Enhanced User Experience:**

- *Smart Homes:* IoT devices in homes provide convenience and energy savings, from smart thermostats and lighting to security systems and voice assistants.

- *Personalization:* IoT data can be used to personalize user experiences in retail, entertainment, and services, increasing customer satisfaction.

4. **Safety and Security:**

- *Surveillance and Monitoring:* IoT-enabled cameras and sensors enhance security and surveillance, reducing crime rates and improving emergency response.

- *Environmental Monitoring:* IoT assists in tracking air quality, water quality, and climate data, contributing to environmental conservation efforts.

5. **Cost Savings:**

   - *Energy Efficiency:* Smart buildings and grids optimize energy consumption, reducing costs and environmental impact.

   - *Predictive Maintenance:* By predicting equipment failures, IoT reduces repair and replacement costs in various industries.

Challenges of IoT:

1. **Security and Privacy:**

   - *Data Breaches:* IoT devices can be vulnerable to hacking and data breaches, potentially exposing sensitive information.

   - *Privacy Concerns:* The constant data collection by IoT devices raises concerns about privacy and surveillance, requiring robust privacy policies and regulations.

2. **Interoperability:**

   - *Fragmentation:* The proliferation of different standards and protocols can lead to compatibility issues, hindering device interoperability and integration.

3. **Scalability:**

- *Data Overload:* Managing and processing the massive volumes of data generated by IoT devices can strain existing infrastructure and analytics capabilities.

4. **Reliability and Downtime:**

- *Dependence on Connectivity:* IoT systems rely on stable connectivity, making them vulnerable to network disruptions and downtime.

- *Device Reliability:* Device failures or malfunctions can disrupt operations, especially in critical applications like healthcare and manufacturing.

5. **Regulatory and Ethical Concerns:**

- *Regulatory Compliance:* IoT must adhere to evolving regulations and standards, which can vary across industries and regions.

- *Ethical Dilemmas:* Balancing innovation with ethical considerations, such as data ownership and consent, presents challenges for IoT stakeholders.

6. **Environmental Impact:**

- *E-Waste:* The disposal of IoT devices contributes to electronic waste, raising sustainability concerns.

- *Energy Consumption:* Some IoT devices may consume substantial energy, offsetting their energy-saving benefits.

7. **Cost and Complexity:**

- *Initial Investment:* Implementing IoT infrastructure and devices can require significant upfront costs.

- *Complexity:* Managing the diverse components of the IoT ecosystem can be complex, necessitating skilled professionals.

In conclusion, the Internet of Things has the potential to transform industries and improve everyday life through automation, data-driven insights, and enhanced experiences. However, the complex challenges it poses, from security and interoperability to privacy and ethical considerations, require careful consideration and proactive solutions. As IoT continues to evolve, striking a balance between reaping its benefits and addressing its challenges will be essential for its continued growth and success.

CHAPTER 2

Introduction to IoT Hardware

The Internet of Things (IoT) is a world of interconnectivity, where the physical and digital realms converge to create a dynamic network of intelligent devices. At the heart of this transformative technology lies IoT hardware, the tangible components that empower everyday objects to become "smart." In this chapter, we embark on a journey into the fascinating world of IoT hardware, exploring the fundamental building blocks that enable objects to sense, communicate, and adapt in a connected ecosystem.

IoT hardware encompasses a diverse range of components, from sensors and microcontrollers to communication modules and processing units. These components work in harmony to bring life to the IoT, giving objects the ability to gather data from their surroundings, transmit it across networks, and respond to changing conditions autonomously. As we delve deeper into this chapter, we will unravel the intricate details of IoT hardware, understanding how it forms the bedrock upon which the Internet of Things stands, driving innovation, efficiency, and transformative change across industries and daily life. Welcome to the world of IoT hardware, where the physical meets the digital, and possibilities abound.

A. Sensors and Actuators in IoT: The Senses and Actions of Things

In the realm of the Internet of Things (IoT), sensors and actuators are the unsung heroes, serving as the eyes, ears, and hands of connected objects. These two critical components form the sensory and responsive foundation of IoT devices, enabling them to perceive their environment, collect data, and take actions based on that data. In this exploration, we delve into the intricate world of sensors and actuators, shedding light on their functionalities, types, and the pivotal roles they play in IoT.

1. Sensors: The Perception of IoT

a. Types of Sensors in IoT:

- **Environmental Sensors:** These sensors monitor various environmental parameters, such as temperature, humidity, air quality, and atmospheric pressure. They are essential for applications like weather monitoring, indoor climate control, and environmental conservation.

- **Motion and Proximity Sensors:** Motion sensors detect movement and changes in motion, while proximity sensors identify the presence of objects within a specified range. These sensors are widely used in security systems, smart lighting, and robotics.

- **Biometric Sensors:** Found in wearable IoT devices, these sensors measure physiological data such as heart rate, blood pressure, skin conductivity, and more. They enable health and fitness tracking, as well as biometric security applications.

- **Image and Video Sensors:** Cameras and imaging sensors capture visual information, making them crucial for surveillance, autonomous vehicles, and facial recognition systems.

- **Position and Location Sensors:** GPS and RFID (Radio-Frequency Identification) sensors provide precise location data, supporting navigation, logistics, asset tracking, and geofencing applications.

b. Functions of Sensors in IoT:

- **Data Collection:** Sensors continuously collect data from their surroundings, converting physical phenomena into electrical signals or digital data.

- **Data Accuracy:** High-quality sensors provide accurate and reliable measurements, ensuring the integrity of collected data.

- **Real-Time Monitoring:** IoT sensors offer real-time monitoring capabilities, enabling timely responses to changing conditions.

- **Event Detection:** Some sensors are designed to detect specific events or conditions, such as motion detection in security systems or gas leak detection in industrial settings.

2. Actuators: The Actions of IoT

Actuators are the counterparts to sensors in IoT devices, providing the means to take physical actions based on data or commands received. They translate digital signals or instructions into tangible movements, operations, or changes in the device's environment.

a. Types of Actuators in IoT:

- **Electric Motors:** Electric actuators are versatile and commonly used in various applications. They can drive mechanical movements, such as opening and closing valves, adjusting positions, or rotating objects.

- **Solenoids:** Solenoid actuators convert electrical energy into linear motion. They are often used in lock mechanisms, automotive applications, and industrial equipment.

- **Piezoelectric Actuators:** These actuators operate on the piezoelectric effect and are used for precise movements and adjustments, such as in nanopositioning and medical devices.

- **Pneumatic and Hydraulic Actuators:** In certain industrial settings, pneumatic and hydraulic actuators are employed to control larger-scale movements and operations.

b. Functions of Actuators in IoT:

- **Automation:** Actuators enable automation by performing actions in response to predefined triggers or commands, reducing the need for human intervention.

- **Control:** Actuators can control physical processes, such as adjusting the position of a valve in a fluid control system or tilting solar panels to optimize sunlight exposure.

- **Feedback Loop:** Actuators often work in tandem with sensors to create feedback loops, where sensor data triggers actuator actions, and the actuator's response is monitored by sensors, ensuring a desired outcome.

3. The Synergy of Sensors and Actuators:

The symbiotic relationship between sensors and actuators is the core of IoT's ability to bridge the physical and digital worlds. Sensors perceive changes in the physical environment, collect data, and transmit it to central systems or other devices. Actuators, on the other hand, receive commands or data and carry out physical actions or adjustments in response.

Examples of Sensor-Actuator Interactions in IoT:

- A temperature sensor detects a rise in room temperature and triggers an actuator to adjust the air conditioner to a more comfortable setting.

- In an autonomous vehicle, a proximity sensor detects an obstacle in the vehicle's path, prompting the actuator to steer the vehicle away from the obstacle.

- In a smart irrigation system, soil moisture sensors inform actuators to release water when the soil is too dry, ensuring optimal plant hydration.

- In industrial automation, sensors detect quality deviations in a production line, and actuators adjust machinery or halt production to maintain product quality.

In conclusion, sensors and actuators are the sensory and responsive elements that breathe life into IoT devices. They empower objects to perceive, collect, and act on data, making IoT's promise of automation, efficiency, and real-time responsiveness a reality. As we delve deeper into the world of IoT applications and solutions in subsequent chapters, we will witness how these components come together to create innovative solutions that address complex challenges across industries and daily life.

B. Microcontrollers and Processors in IoT: The Brains of Connected Things

In the intricate web of the Internet of Things (IoT), microcontrollers and processors are the central nervous system, responsible for processing data, executing commands, and making intelligent decisions. These tiny yet powerful components are the driving force behind IoT devices, enabling them to gather information from sensors, communicate with other devices, and perform actions autonomously. In this exploration, we delve into the world of microcontrollers and processors, uncovering their functionalities, types, and the pivotal roles they play in the IoT ecosystem.

1. Microcontrollers: The Miniature Computers of IoT

Microcontrollers are compact, integrated computing devices that combine a processor (CPU), memory, input/output interfaces, and often a real-time clock into a single chip. They are designed to handle specific tasks efficiently and with minimal power consumption, making them ideal for IoT applications.

a. Functions of Microcontrollers in IoT:

- **Data Processing:** Microcontrollers process data collected by sensors, making sense of raw measurements and converting them into meaningful information.

- **Control:** Microcontrollers are responsible for controlling actuators, enabling IoT devices to perform actions based on sensor data or user commands.

- **Connectivity:** Many microcontrollers have built-in communication interfaces (e.g., Wi-Fi, Bluetooth, Zigbee) that allow IoT devices to connect to networks and communicate with other devices or cloud services.

- **Power Management:** Microcontrollers are designed for low power consumption, crucial for battery-powered IoT devices and energy-efficient operation.

b. Types of Microcontrollers:

- **Arduino:** Arduino is a popular open-source platform for prototyping IoT devices. It uses a variety of microcontroller chips, with the ATmega series being a common choice.

- **Raspberry Pi:** While technically a single-board computer, the Raspberry Pi is often used in IoT projects due to its versatility, processing power, and extensive community support.

- **ESP8266 and ESP32:** These microcontrollers from Espressif Systems are widely used in IoT applications due to their built-in Wi-Fi and Bluetooth capabilities.

- **ARM Cortex-M Series:** ARM-based microcontrollers are known for their energy efficiency and are commonly used in IoT devices.

2. Processors: The Computational Powerhouses of IoT

Processors in the context of IoT typically refer to more powerful central processing units (CPUs) compared to microcontrollers. These processors can handle complex tasks, run full operating systems, and are often used in edge computing devices and gateways.

a. Functions of Processors in IoT:

- **Advanced Computing:** Processors can execute complex algorithms, making them suitable for edge AI, image processing, and advanced analytics.

- **Operating Systems:** Processors can run full-fledged operating systems like Linux, enabling multi-tasking and supporting a wide range of applications.

- **Gateway and Edge Computing:** In IoT architectures, processors are commonly used in gateways that aggregate data from multiple sensors and devices, perform local processing, and transmit relevant data to the cloud.

- **Security:** Processors can handle advanced security protocols and encryption, essential for securing IoT data and communication.

b. Types of Processors:

- **ARM Cortex-A Series:** These processors are commonly found in smartphones and tablets and are often used in IoT gateways and edge computing devices.

- **Intel and AMD x86 CPUs:** Traditional x86 processors are used in some IoT applications, particularly those requiring compatibility with existing software and infrastructure.

- **NVIDIA GPUs:** Graphics processing units (GPUs) from NVIDIA are used in edge AI and machine learning applications within IoT devices.

3. The Synergy of Microcontrollers and Processors:

In many IoT systems, microcontrollers and processors work together in a complementary fashion. Microcontrollers handle sensor data collection, basic processing, and control, while processors handle more complex tasks, such as data analytics, machine learning, and communication with the cloud. This division of labor optimizes power consumption, performance, and responsiveness in IoT devices.

Examples of Microcontroller-Processor Synergy in IoT:

- In a smart security camera, a microcontroller manages real-time motion detection and image capture, while a processor performs facial recognition and stores video footage.

- In a wearable fitness tracker, a microcontroller collects sensor data for heart rate and steps, while a processor runs algorithms to analyze fitness metrics and syncs data to a smartphone app.

- In an industrial IoT system, microcontrollers in sensors monitor equipment conditions, while processors in edge gateways perform predictive maintenance analysis and send alerts to maintenance teams.

Conclusion:

Microcontrollers and processors are the computational brains of IoT devices, orchestrating the collection of data, execution of commands, and autonomous decision-making. The choice between microcontrollers and processors depends on the specific requirements of an IoT application, including power efficiency, processing power, and connectivity options. As IoT continues to evolve, these components will play an increasingly pivotal role in shaping the capabilities and intelligence of connected things, driving innovation and efficiency across industries and domains.

C. Communication Protocols in IoT: Enabling Connectivity

Communication protocols are the digital languages spoken by devices in the Internet of Things (IoT) ecosystem, allowing them to exchange data, commands, and information seamlessly. These protocols play a vital role in determining the range, power efficiency, data throughput, and suitability for various IoT applications. In this exploration, we delve into some of the most common communication protocols used in IoT, including Wi-Fi, Bluetooth, LoRa, and cellular technologies.

1. Wi-Fi (IEEE 802.11):

a. Features:

- **High Data Throughput:** Wi-Fi offers high-speed data transfer, making it suitable for applications requiring rapid data exchange, such as video streaming or real-time monitoring.

- **Short to Medium Range:** Wi-Fi typically operates within a limited range, making it ideal for home automation, office environments, and local area networks (LANs).

- **Infrastructure-Based:** Wi-Fi networks are typically infrastructure-based, relying on access points or routers to provide connectivity to IoT devices.

- **Power Consumption:** Traditional Wi-Fi can consume relatively more power compared to low-power IoT communication protocols, which can limit battery life in IoT devices.

b. Use Cases:

- **Smart Homes:** Wi-Fi is commonly used in smart home devices such as smart speakers, security cameras, thermostats, and appliances due to its high data throughput.

- **Enterprise IoT:** Wi-Fi is prevalent in office environments for connecting IoT devices like printers, access control systems, and inventory tracking devices.

2. Bluetooth:

a. Features:

- **Low Power:** Bluetooth Low Energy (BLE) is a low-power variant of Bluetooth, making it suitable for battery-operated IoT devices with long battery life.

- **Short Range:** Bluetooth operates within a short range, making it ideal for applications like wearables, proximity sensing, and indoor navigation.

- **Point-to-Point and Mesh Networking:** Bluetooth supports both point-to-point and mesh networking, allowing devices to communicate directly or form mesh networks for extended range and redundancy.

b. Use Cases:

- **Wearables:** Bluetooth is commonly used in smartwatches, fitness trackers, and health monitoring devices due to its low power consumption and short-range connectivity.

- **Beacons:** Bluetooth beacons are used for location-based services, marketing, and indoor navigation.

3. LoRa (Long Range):

a. Features:

- **Ultra-Low Power:** LoRa devices can operate on battery power for extended periods, making them suitable for remote and battery-operated IoT applications.

- **Long Range:** LoRa offers long-range communication, often spanning several kilometers, making it ideal for applications like precision agriculture, environmental monitoring, and smart cities.

- **Low Data Rate:** LoRa's data rate is relatively low compared to Wi-Fi or cellular technologies, making it suitable for applications that do not require high-speed data transfer.

b. Use Cases:

- **Agriculture:** LoRa is used in precision agriculture for remote monitoring of soil conditions, crop health, and weather data.

- **Smart Cities:** LoRa is employed for various smart city applications, including smart parking, waste management, and environmental monitoring.

4. Cellular Technologies (2G, 3G, 4G, and 5G):

a. Features:

- **Wide Coverage:** Cellular networks offer extensive coverage, making them suitable for IoT devices in remote or wide-area deployments.

- **High Data Throughput:** 4G and 5G cellular networks provide high-speed data transfer, enabling applications like autonomous vehicles and high-definition video surveillance.

- **Scalability:** Cellular networks are highly scalable and can support a large number of IoT devices simultaneously.

b. Use Cases:

- **Asset Tracking:** Cellular IoT is used for tracking assets in logistics, transportation, and supply chain management.

- **Smart Grids:** Utilities use cellular networks for managing smart grids and monitoring energy infrastructure.

Conclusion:

Communication protocols in IoT serve as the lifeline that connects devices, enabling them to collect, transmit, and receive data. The choice of protocol depends on factors such as range, power consumption, data throughput, and application requirements. As IoT continues to evolve, new communication protocols and standards, especially those designed for low-power and long-range applications, will continue to emerge, expanding the possibilities for connected devices and enabling innovative solutions across industries and domains.

D. Power Management in IoT: Sustaining Connectivity and Efficiency

Power management is a cornerstone of Internet of Things (IoT) design, essential for ensuring that connected devices can operate reliably, efficiently, and sustainably. In the world of IoT, where devices range from battery-powered sensors to energy-hungry gateways, managing power consumption is crucial to extending battery life, reducing operational costs, and minimizing environmental impact. In this exploration, we delve into the multifaceted realm of power management in IoT, examining the challenges, strategies, and technologies that enable devices to strike the right balance between functionality and power efficiency.

1. Power Challenges in IoT:

IoT devices encounter a myriad of power-related challenges due to their diverse applications and deployment scenarios:

- **Limited Energy Resources:** Battery-powered IoT devices face constraints on the amount of energy they can store and use. Energy harvesting (e.g., from solar or kinetic sources) may provide renewable power but often at a limited rate.

- **Energy-Efficiency vs. Performance:** Balancing the need for device performance with energy efficiency is a constant challenge. High-performance operations may drain batteries quickly.

- **Remote and Unattended Deployment:** Many IoT devices are deployed in remote or inaccessible locations, making battery replacement or recharging difficult and costly.

- **Variability in Workloads:** IoT devices often have variable workloads, which can affect their power consumption patterns. For example, a sensor may transmit data sporadically, resulting in bursty power usage.

2. Power Management Strategies:

To address these challenges, IoT devices employ various power management strategies:

- **Low-Power Hardware:** Devices are designed with low-power components, such as microcontrollers, sensors, and communication modules, to minimize energy consumption during both active and sleep states.

- **Duty Cycling:** Devices operate in low-power sleep modes when not actively performing tasks and wake up periodically to perform actions like data sensing, processing, or transmission. This reduces overall energy consumption.

- **Adaptive Behavior:** IoT devices adjust their behavior based on power availability and workload. For example, a device may lower its sensor sampling frequency when battery levels are low.

- **Energy Harvesting:** In certain applications, IoT devices leverage energy from ambient sources like solar panels, vibrations, or temperature differentials to recharge or extend battery life.

3. Power Management Technologies:

Several technologies and techniques are used to optimize power management in IoT:

- **Sleep Modes:** IoT devices can enter sleep modes where non-essential components are turned off or placed in a low-power state. Wake-up mechanisms (e.g., timers or interrupts) bring the device back to an active state when needed.

- **Energy-Efficient Communication Protocols:** Low-power communication protocols like Bluetooth Low Energy (BLE) and LoRaWAN minimize energy consumption during data transmission.

- **Dynamic Voltage and Frequency Scaling (DVFS):** This technique adjusts the voltage and clock frequency of the processor based on workload, reducing power consumption during periods of lower demand.

- **Power Gating:** Power gating involves completely shutting down power to certain device components when they are not in use, preventing any power leakage.

- **Energy Storage:** Advanced energy storage solutions, including supercapacitors and advanced batteries, can store energy more efficiently and tolerate frequent charge-discharge cycles.

4. Software-Based Power Optimization:

Power management is not limited to hardware; software plays a critical role as well:

- **Optimized Algorithms:** IoT device software can incorporate efficient algorithms for data compression, aggregation, and filtering to minimize the amount of data sent and processed, reducing energy consumption.

- **Predictive Analytics:** Machine learning and predictive analytics can optimize device behavior based on historical data and predicted usage patterns.

- **Firmware Updates:** Device manufacturers can release firmware updates to improve power management and energy efficiency.

5. Real-Time Monitoring and Management:

Remote monitoring and management tools allow organizations to track the power status and performance of IoT devices, enabling proactive maintenance and energy-saving strategies.

Conclusion:

Power management is a fundamental consideration in the design and operation of IoT devices. By implementing efficient hardware, software, and strategies, IoT deployments can achieve prolonged battery life, reduced operational costs, and a smaller environmental footprint. As IoT continues to expand and diversify across industries, effective power management will remain a critical element in realizing the full potential of connected devices.

E. Edge Computing Devices in IoT: Bringing Intelligence Closer to Data

Edge computing devices are the workhorses of the Internet of Things (IoT), bringing computational power and intelligence closer to where data is generated. These devices play a pivotal role in processing, analyzing, and acting on data locally, reducing latency, conserving bandwidth, and enhancing real-time decision-making. In this exploration, we delve into the world of edge computing devices, examining their functionalities, use cases, and the impact they have on IoT applications across various domains.

1. The Role of Edge Computing Devices:

Edge computing devices bridge the gap between IoT devices at the network's edge and centralized cloud resources. Their primary functions include:

- **Data Processing:** Edge devices process data locally, performing computations, data filtering, and analysis without the need to send data to a remote cloud server. This reduces latency and conserves network bandwidth.

- **Real-Time Decision-Making:** By processing data locally, edge devices enable rapid, real-time decision-making, critical for applications like autonomous vehicles, industrial automation, and healthcare monitoring.

- **Local Storage:** Edge devices often include storage capabilities, allowing them to store and manage data locally, which is valuable for offline operation and data continuity in unreliable network environments.

- **Security:** Data processed and stored at the edge is inherently more secure as it doesn't traverse networks, reducing the risk of data breaches and ensuring data privacy.

2. Types of Edge Computing Devices:

Edge computing devices come in various forms, depending on the application requirements:

- **Edge Servers:** These are more robust computing devices that provide significant processing power and storage capacity. They are commonly used in industrial settings, smart cities, and retail for local data processing and analytics.

- **Gateway Devices:** Gateways serve as intermediaries between IoT devices and the cloud. They often aggregate data from multiple sensors and devices, preprocess it, and transmit only relevant information to the cloud. This reduces cloud data transfer costs and latency.

- **Edge Routers:** Edge routers are specialized devices that route data traffic at the network edge, often used in industrial and telecommunications applications.

- **Industrial PCs:** In industrial settings, rugged industrial PCs act as edge computing devices to control machinery, process data locally, and ensure real-time operation.

- **Edge AI Devices:** Edge AI devices are equipped with specialized hardware, such as GPUs and TPUs, to perform machine learning and AI inferencing locally. These are used in applications like computer vision, natural language processing, and predictive maintenance.

3. Use Cases and Applications:

Edge computing devices find applications across various industries and domains:

- **Industrial IoT (IIoT):** In manufacturing and industrial settings, edge computing devices enable real-time monitoring of machinery, predictive maintenance, and quality control.

- **Smart Cities:** Edge devices support applications like smart traffic management, waste management, and environmental monitoring, ensuring efficient urban operations.

- **Healthcare:** In healthcare, edge computing devices enable real-time monitoring of patients, analysis of medical images, and the processing of data from wearable devices.

- **Retail:** Retail stores use edge devices for inventory management, customer tracking, and personalized marketing in real-time.

- **Autonomous Vehicles:** Edge computing devices in autonomous vehicles process sensor data for real-time decision-making, ensuring safety and navigation.

4. Edge Computing and IoT Ecosystem:

Edge computing devices are integral components of the

broader IoT ecosystem. They work in synergy with sensors, actuators, and communication technologies to create responsive and intelligent IoT solutions. Data collected by sensors is preprocessed and analyzed at the edge, and only relevant information is transmitted to centralized systems for further analysis or storage.

Conclusion:

Edge computing devices are pivotal in enabling real-time processing, low-latency decision-making, and data security in IoT applications. They empower organizations to harness the full potential of IoT by bringing computational power closer to the data source. As IoT continues to evolve, edge computing devices will remain at the forefront, driving innovation and efficiency across industries and domains, and ensuring that IoT delivers on its promise of transformative technology.

CHAPTER 3

Introduction to IoT Connectivity

In the vast and interconnected landscape of the Internet of Things (IoT), connectivity is the thread that weaves together a tapestry of devices, sensors, and systems into a seamless network. IoT connectivity encompasses the various means by which these smart objects communicate, share data, and collaborate to deliver real-time insights, automation, and efficiency. This chapter embarks on a journey into the multifaceted realm of IoT connectivity, exploring the diverse technologies and protocols that bind the IoT ecosystem together and enable the exchange of information on a global scale. From wired connections to wireless networks and emerging standards, this chapter unravels the intricate web of IoT connectivity, shedding light on its significance, challenges, and transformative potential in our increasingly connected world. Welcome to the realm of IoT connectivity, where the future is defined by the power to communicate and collaborate across boundaries, unlocking new possibilities and reshaping industries and daily life.

A. Wired and Wireless Communication in IoT: Bridging the Connectivity Divide

Wired and wireless communication technologies form the backbone of the Internet of Things (IoT), enabling devices and sensors to connect, share data, and collaborate in various applications. These communication methods come with their own strengths and limitations, making them suitable for different use cases within the diverse IoT ecosystem. In this exploration, we delve into the world of wired and wireless communication in IoT, examining their characteristics, applications, and how they contribute to the seamless interconnectivity of IoT devices.

1. Wired Communication:

a. Characteristics:

- **Reliability:** Wired connections, such as Ethernet and Power over Ethernet (PoE), are known for their high reliability and stable data transmission, making them suitable for critical applications.

- **Security:** Wired connections are generally considered more secure than wireless counterparts because they are less susceptible to interception and interference.

- **High Bandwidth:** Wired connections typically offer higher bandwidth, making them suitable for applications requiring large data transfers.

b. Applications:

- **Industrial IoT (IIoT):** In manufacturing and industrial settings, Ethernet-based wired communication is prevalent for connecting machinery, sensors, and control systems.

- **Smart Buildings:** Wired connections are used for building automation systems, including access control, HVAC, and lighting.

- **Data Centers:** Data centers rely on high-speed wired connections for server communication and data storage.

2. Wireless Communication:

a. Characteristics:

- **Mobility:** Wireless communication offers the advantage of mobility, allowing IoT devices to move freely within a network.

- **Flexibility:** Wireless communication is flexible and adaptable, making it suitable for dynamic and evolving IoT environments.

- **Scalability:** Wireless networks can easily accommodate a growing number of IoT devices, making them scalable and cost-effective.

b. Types of Wireless Communication:

- **Wi-Fi (IEEE 802.11):** Wi-Fi provides high-speed wireless connectivity over short to medium ranges, making it suitable for applications like smart homes and offices.

- **Bluetooth:** Bluetooth is commonly used for short-range connectivity between IoT devices, such as wearable devices, smartphones, and peripherals.

- **Cellular Networks:** Cellular networks (2G, 3G, 4G, and 5G) offer wide-area coverage, making them suitable for IoT applications that require connectivity in remote or mobile environments.

- **LoRaWAN:** LoRaWAN is a low-power, long-range wireless communication protocol suitable for applications like agriculture, environmental monitoring, and smart cities.

- **Zigbee and Z-Wave:** These protocols are designed for low-power, low-data-rate communication in smart home and building automation.

c. Applications:

- **Smart Agriculture:** Wireless sensors and actuators in agriculture rely on long-range wireless communication technologies like LoRaWAN to monitor soil conditions, weather, and irrigation.

- **Healthcare:** Wearable medical devices use Bluetooth to connect with smartphones and relay health data to healthcare providers.

- **Smart Cities:** Wireless networks enable smart city applications such as smart traffic management, waste management, and environmental monitoring.

3. Hybrid Connectivity:

In some IoT applications, a combination of wired and wireless communication is used to optimize connectivity. For instance, a wired Ethernet connection may be used for critical data transfer, while Wi-Fi provides mobility within a local area.

4. Challenges and Considerations:

- **Security:** Wireless networks require robust security measures to prevent unauthorized access and data breaches.

- **Interference:** Wireless communication can be susceptible to interference from other devices and electromagnetic signals.

- **Power Consumption:** Wireless IoT devices need to manage power efficiently to prolong battery life.

Conclusion:

Wired and wireless communication technologies are the veins and arteries of the IoT ecosystem, connecting devices, sensors, and systems to enable seamless data exchange and collaboration. The choice between wired and wireless communication depends on factors like range, reliability, security, and bandwidth, as well as the specific requirements of IoT applications. As IoT continues to evolve and diversify, the coexistence of various communication methods ensures that the connectivity needs of a wide range of industries and domains are met, fostering innovation, efficiency, and transformative change.

B. IoT Networking Technologies: Unleashing Connectivity Possibilities

IoT networking technologies are the lifelines that empower connected devices to communicate, share data, and collaborate across the Internet of Things (IoT) landscape. These technologies encompass a wide spectrum, each tailored to specific use cases and requirements, whether it's ultra-fast, low-latency communication for autonomous vehicles or low-power, long-range connectivity for remote environmental sensors. In this exploration, we delve into key IoT networking technologies, shedding light on their characteristics, applications, and pivotal roles within the ever-expanding IoT ecosystem.

1. 5G (Fifth Generation):

a. Characteristics:

- **High-Speed Data:** 5G offers unparalleled data speeds, low latency, and high capacity, making it suitable for applications that demand real-time data transmission, such as augmented reality (AR), virtual reality (VR), and autonomous vehicles.

- **Massive IoT:** 5G supports Massive Machine-Type Communications (mMTC), enabling a vast number of low-power IoT devices to be connected to a single network infrastructure.

- **Low Latency:** Ultra-low latency in 5G networks is vital for applications like remote surgery, industrial automation, and autonomous vehicles.

b. Applications:

- **Autonomous Vehicles:** 5G enables real-time vehicle-to-vehicle (V2V) and vehicle-to-infrastructure (V2I) communication, crucial for the safety and coordination of autonomous vehicles.

- **Smart Cities:** 5G networks support smart city applications like traffic management, environmental monitoring, and public safety.

2. NB-IoT (Narrowband IoT):

a. Characteristics:

- **Low Power:** NB-IoT is designed for low-power, wide-area IoT applications, ensuring long battery life for connected devices.

- **Deep Coverage:** It provides deep indoor and underground coverage, making it suitable for applications in remote and challenging environments.

- **Reliability:** NB-IoT offers reliable data transmission, which is essential for applications like asset tracking and smart meters.

b. Applications:

- **Smart Metering:** NB-IoT is commonly used for smart gas and water meters, allowing remote monitoring and management.

- **Agriculture:** In precision agriculture, NB-IoT is used for soil monitoring, weather stations, and livestock tracking.

3. Zigbee:

a. Characteristics:

- **Low-Power:** Zigbee is designed for low-power, short-range communication, making it ideal for battery-operated devices like smart home sensors and controls.

- **Mesh Networking:** Zigbee devices can form self-healing mesh networks, extending the range and improving reliability.

- **Interoperability:** Zigbee Alliance ensures device interoperability, enabling various manufacturers to create compatible devices.

b. Applications:

- **Smart Homes:** Zigbee is widely used for smart home devices, including smart lighting, door locks, and thermostats.

- **Industrial Automation:** In industrial settings, Zigbee is used for process control, asset tracking, and equipment monitoring.

4. LoRaWAN (Long Range Wide Area Network):

a. Characteristics:

- **Long Range:** LoRaWAN offers long-range communication, covering several kilometers in rural areas and urban environments.

- **Low Power:** LoRaWAN devices are energy-efficient, making them suitable for remote monitoring and tracking applications.

- **Low Data Rate:** It operates at low data rates, making it

3

33333

suitable for applications that don't require high-speed data transfer.

b. Applications:

- **Smart Agriculture:** LoRaWAN is used for soil moisture monitoring, weather stations, and livestock tracking in agriculture.

- **Smart Cities:** LoRaWAN supports smart city applications like waste management, parking, and environmental monitoring.

5. Sigfox:

a. Characteristics:

- **Ultra Low-Power:** Sigfox devices consume minimal power, extending the battery life of connected devices.

- **Global Network:** Sigfox operates a global network for low-power, long-range IoT connectivity.

- **Cost-Efficient:** Sigfox offers cost-efficient connectivity for applications like asset tracking and remote monitoring.

b. Applications:

- **Asset Tracking:** Sigfox is used for tracking assets in logistics, transportation, and supply chain management.

- **Environmental Monitoring:** Sigfox supports environmental monitoring applications such as air quality and water quality monitoring.

Conclusion:

IoT networking technologies are the arteries of the IoT ecosystem, delivering connectivity possibilities that cater to the diverse needs of various industries and applications. The choice of networking technology depends on factors like range, power consumption, data throughput, and the specific requirements of IoT deployments. As IoT continues to evolve, the coexistence of multiple networking technologies ensures that connected devices can thrive in various environments, fostering innovation, efficiency, and transformative change across industries and domains.

C. IoT Device Management: Orchestrating the Connected Ecosystem

IoT device management is the backbone of a seamless and efficient Internet of Things (IoT) ecosystem. It involves the monitoring, provisioning, configuration, security, and maintenance of a multitude of devices, sensors, and gateways spread across various networks and locations. Effective device management is essential for ensuring the reliability, security, and scalability of IoT deployments. In this exploration, we dive into the intricate world of IoT device management, unveiling its importance, key components, challenges, and strategies that enable organizations to harness the full potential of connected devices.

1. The Significance of IoT Device Management:

IoT device management serves as the foundation for a well-orchestrated IoT infrastructure:

- **Reliability:** It ensures the reliable operation of devices, reducing downtime and optimizing the performance of the IoT ecosystem.

- **Scalability:** Device management facilitates the onboarding and management of a growing number of devices, ensuring seamless scalability.

- **Security:** Proper management is essential for implementing robust security measures, protecting devices, data, and the overall network.

- **Remote Control:** It enables remote monitoring and control of IoT devices, reducing the need for physical intervention.

2. Key Components of IoT Device Management:

IoT device management encompasses several critical components:

- **Device Provisioning:** This involves adding devices to the network, configuring initial settings, and ensuring secure authentication and authorization.

- **Configuration Management:** It includes remotely configuring device parameters, updating firmware, and ensuring devices operate optimally.

- **Monitoring and Diagnostics:** Real-time monitoring of device health, performance, and diagnostics is crucial for identifying issues and taking proactive measures.

- **Security:** Device management is essential for enforcing security policies, patching vulnerabilities, and responding to security threats.

- **Firmware and Software Updates:** Regular updates to device firmware and software are vital for adding features, fixing bugs, and enhancing security.

- **Data Management:** Managing data generated by IoT devices, including storage, processing, and transmission, is a key aspect of device management.

3. Challenges in IoT Device Management:

IoT device management is not without its challenges:

- **Device Diversity:** IoT ecosystems often consist of a diverse range of devices with varying capabilities and communication protocols.

- **Security:** Ensuring the security of IoT devices and data in a constantly evolving threat landscape is a significant challenge.

- **Scalability:** Managing a large number of devices and gateways in a scalable manner requires efficient processes and tools.

- **Interoperability:** Ensuring interoperability between devices from different manufacturers can be complex.

- **Data Management:** Managing the vast amount of data generated by IoT devices and extracting actionable insights can be challenging.

4. IoT Device Management Strategies:

To overcome these challenges, organizations adopt various strategies:

- **Device Registration and Onboarding:** Standardized procedures for registering and onboarding devices simplify the management process.

- **Remote Monitoring and Control:** Implementing tools and platforms for remote monitoring, diagnostics, and control streamlines device management.

- **Data Analytics:** Leveraging data analytics and machine learning to gain insights from device data helps in predictive maintenance and proactive issue resolution.

- **Security Protocols:** Robust security protocols, including encryption, authentication, and intrusion detection, are crucial for device protection.

- **APIs and Standards:** Adherence to industry standards and open APIs facilitates interoperability between devices and platforms.

5. IoT Device Management Platforms:

IoT device management platforms, such as Microsoft Azure IoT Hub, AWS IoT Core, and Google Cloud IoT Core, provide centralized tools and services for device management, security, and data processing. These platforms simplify device onboarding, monitoring, and control, making it easier for organizations to manage their IoT deployments effectively.

Conclusion:

IoT device management is the linchpin that holds together the sprawling IoT ecosystem. As the number of connected devices continues to grow, the importance of efficient and secure device management cannot be overstated. By adopting robust strategies, leveraging IoT device management platforms, and staying vigilant in the face of evolving challenges, organizations can ensure the reliability, scalability, and security of their IoT deployments, unlocking the full potential of the connected world.

D. IoT Security Considerations: Safeguarding the Connected World

IoT security is a paramount concern as the Internet of Things (IoT) continues to proliferate across industries and domains. The interconnected nature of IoT devices, coupled with their diverse applications, makes them vulnerable targets for cyber threats and data breaches. Effective IoT security measures are essential to protect devices, data, and networks from potential attacks and ensure the privacy, integrity, and reliability of IoT deployments. In this exploration, we delve into the multifaceted world of IoT security, examining its challenges, key considerations, and strategies for safeguarding the connected world.

1. IoT Security Challenges:

Securing IoT poses unique challenges:

- **Device Diversity:** IoT ecosystems consist of a wide variety of devices, ranging from sensors and actuators to gateways and edge devices, each with varying levels of processing power and security capabilities.

- **Network Complexity:** IoT networks span multiple protocols, standards, and communication technologies, making them susceptible to vulnerabilities at different layers.

- **Data Privacy:** IoT devices generate vast amounts of data, including sensitive information. Ensuring data privacy and protection is critical.

- **Lifecycle Management:** Managing the security of IoT devices throughout their lifecycle, including provisioning, updates, and end-of-life, is a complex task.

- **Scalability:** IoT deployments can scale to include millions of devices, necessitating security solutions that can handle this magnitude.

2. Key IoT Security Considerations:

Effective IoT security encompasses several critical considerations:

- **Device Authentication:** Ensuring that only authorized devices can connect to the network is fundamental. Authentication mechanisms like certificates, tokens, and biometrics are commonly used.

- **Data Encryption:** Data should be encrypted during transmission and storage to prevent unauthorized access. Protocols like TLS/SSL and AES encryption are vital.

- **Access Control:** Implementing access control mechanisms restricts device and user access to specific resources, preventing unauthorized actions.

- **Firmware Updates:** Regularly updating device firmware is essential to patch vulnerabilities and improve security. Secure over-the-air (OTA) updates are common.

- **Security Monitoring:** Real-time monitoring of device and network behavior can help identify abnormal activities and potential security threats.

- **Physical Security:** Physical security measures protect IoT devices from tampering and unauthorized access. This is crucial in applications like industrial control systems.

- **Privacy Protection:** IoT systems should respect user privacy by collecting and handling data in compliance with privacy regulations like GDPR.

3. IoT Security Strategies:

To address these considerations, organizations adopt various security strategies:

- **Security by Design:** Building security into IoT devices and systems from the ground up, rather than as an afterthought, is crucial.

- **Network Segmentation:** Segmenting IoT networks from critical infrastructure can limit the impact of potential breaches.

- **Zero Trust Architecture:** Zero trust principles assume that threats may exist both inside and outside the network and require continuous verification of device trustworthiness.

- **Security Standards:** Adhering to industry-specific security standards and best practices, such as ISO/IEC 27001 and NIST Cybersecurity Framework, can help establish a strong security foundation.

- **Security Analytics:** Leveraging machine learning and AI for anomaly detection can enhance security monitoring and threat detection.

4. IoT Security Technologies:

Various technologies are used to enhance IoT security:

- **Blockchain:** Blockchain technology provides a tamper-proof and transparent ledger, ensuring data integrity and traceability.

- **Identity and Access Management (IAM):** IAM solutions enable centralized control over device and user access to IoT resources.

- **Security Information and Event Management (SIEM):** SIEM systems collect, analyze, and correlate security data from IoT devices and networks, helping detect and respond to threats.

- **Security Orchestration, Automation, and Response (SOAR):** SOAR solutions automate security incident response processes, improving efficiency and reducing response times.

5. IoT Security Regulations:

Governments and regulatory bodies are increasingly introducing IoT security regulations and standards to ensure the protection of consumers and data. Organizations must stay compliant with these regulations to avoid legal and financial consequences.

Conclusion:

IoT security is a multifaceted challenge that requires comprehensive strategies, technologies, and ongoing vigilance. As IoT continues to grow and evolve, so too will the threats and vulnerabilities. By prioritizing security from the outset, staying abreast of the latest security developments, and implementing robust security measures, organizations can harness the transformative potential of IoT while mitigating the associated risks, ultimately safeguarding the connected world.

CHAPTER 4

IoT Data Management

In the vast landscape of the Internet of Things (IoT), data reigns supreme as the lifeblood that powers intelligent decision-making, automation, and innovation. IoT devices generate a torrent of data, ranging from sensor readings and environmental metrics to user interactions and machine insights. Effective IoT data management is the key to harnessing this data deluge, transforming raw information into actionable insights, and driving meaningful outcomes across various industries and applications. In this exploration, we embark on a journey into the realm of IoT data management, unveiling its significance, challenges, strategies, and the pivotal role it plays in shaping the future of connected ecosystems. Welcome to the world of IoT data management, where data is the currency that fuels the engine of innovation and progress.

A. Data Collection and Streaming in IoT: Unleashing Real-Time Insights

Data collection and streaming are the lifeblood of the Internet of Things (IoT). These processes facilitate the continuous flow of information from sensors, devices, and systems, enabling real-time monitoring, analysis, and decision-making. In the IoT ecosystem, where data drives innovation and efficiency across various domains, understanding the intricacies of data collection and streaming is paramount. In this exploration, we delve into the world of data collection and streaming in IoT, unveiling their importance, techniques, challenges, and the transformative potential they hold in shaping the connected world.

1. Data Collection in IoT:

a. Importance:

Data collection is the foundation of IoT. It involves the capture and retrieval of information from various sources, including sensors, devices, and edge computing nodes. The importance of data collection lies in its ability to provide:

- **Visibility:** Data collection offers visibility into the physical and digital world, allowing organizations to monitor processes, environments, and assets in real time.

- **Insights:** Data collected from sensors and devices can be transformed into actionable insights, enabling informed decision-making and predictive maintenance.

- **Automation:** Data collection supports automation by providing the necessary inputs for control systems to respond to changing conditions.

b. Techniques:

Data collection in IoT employs various techniques:

- **Sensor Technologies:** Sensors are the primary data collection devices in IoT, and they come in diverse forms, including temperature sensors, motion detectors, cameras, and more.

- **Communication Protocols:** Data collected by sensors is transmitted to central systems using communication protocols like MQTT, CoAP, HTTP, and custom protocols designed for specific use cases.

- **Edge Computing:** Edge computing devices process data locally, enabling data reduction and filtering before transmitting it to central servers, reducing latency and bandwidth usage.

2. Data Streaming in IoT:

a. Importance:

Data streaming is the process of transmitting real-time data continuously from source to destination. In IoT, data streaming plays a critical role by providing:

- **Real-Time Insights:** Data streaming enables organizations to access and analyze data as it's generated, allowing for real-time decision-making and immediate action.

- **Analytics:** Streaming data can be analyzed using complex algorithms and machine learning models to identify patterns, anomalies, and trends in real time.

- **Synchronization:** Data streaming ensures that data is synchronized across all parts of the IoT ecosystem, providing a single source of truth.

b. Technologies:

Several technologies are used for data streaming in IoT:

- **Apache Kafka:** Kafka is a popular open-source streaming platform that can handle high-throughput, real-time data streams.

- **Apache Flink:** Flink is a stream processing framework used for real-time data analytics and processing.

- **MQTT and CoAP:** These lightweight messaging protocols support real-time data streaming in IoT applications.

- **Custom Streaming Solutions:** Organizations often develop custom data streaming solutions tailored to their specific needs and infrastructure.

3. Challenges in Data Collection and Streaming:

Data collection and streaming in IoT come with their own set of challenges:

- **Scalability:** Scaling data collection to handle a growing number of devices and sensors can be complex and resource-intensive.

- **Data Quality:** Ensuring data accuracy, consistency, and reliability is challenging, especially when dealing with diverse data sources.

- **Latency:** Reducing data transmission and processing latency is essential for applications that require real-time responsiveness.

- **Security:** Protecting data during collection and transmission is crucial to prevent data breaches and unauthorized access.

4. Use Cases:

Data collection and streaming are essential in numerous IoT use cases, including:

- **Smart Cities:** Real-time data from sensors and cameras is streamed to central systems to monitor traffic, air quality, and energy consumption.

- **Manufacturing:** IoT sensors collect data on machine health and production quality, which is streamed for predictive maintenance and process optimization.

- **Healthcare:** Wearable devices continuously collect and

stream patient data for remote monitoring and timely interventions.

Conclusion:

Data collection and streaming are the dynamic processes that fuel the IoT ecosystem, enabling real-time insights, automation, and innovation across various industries and applications. By understanding the importance, techniques, challenges, and technologies involved in data collection and streaming, organizations can harness the transformative potential of IoT, uncovering new possibilities and reshaping the way they operate in an increasingly connected world.

B. Data Storage in IoT: Cloud, Edge, and Fog Solutions

Data storage is a fundamental component of the Internet of Things (IoT) ecosystem, and it plays a critical role in managing the vast amounts of data generated by IoT devices and sensors. In the IoT landscape, data can be stored in various locations, including the cloud, edge, and fog, each with its own set of advantages and use cases. This exploration delves into the intricacies of data storage in IoT, exploring the significance, characteristics, and deployment strategies for cloud, edge, and fog storage solutions.

1. Cloud Data Storage:

a. Significance:

Cloud data storage involves storing IoT-generated data in remote data centers operated by cloud service providers. It offers several advantages:

- **Scalability:** Cloud storage can easily scale to accommodate massive amounts of data, making it suitable for applications with high data volume.

- **Accessibility:** Data stored in the cloud is accessible from anywhere with an internet connection, enabling remote monitoring and analysis.

- **Cost-Efficiency:** Cloud storage often follows a pay-as-you-go model, which can be cost-effective for organizations as it eliminates the need for significant upfront hardware investments.

b. Use Cases:

Cloud storage is ideal for various IoT use cases, such as:

- **Big Data Analytics:** Storing vast amounts of IoT data for later analysis and insights.

- **Historical Data:** Archiving historical data for compliance or long-term analysis.

- **Cross-Device Integration:** Centralizing data from multiple IoT devices for unified processing.

2. Edge Data Storage:

a. Significance:

Edge data storage involves storing IoT data on local devices or gateways, closer to where the data is generated. It offers several advantages:

- **Low Latency:** Edge storage reduces latency, making it suitable for applications requiring real-time or near-real-time data processing.

- **Privacy and Compliance:** Storing sensitive data locally can address privacy and compliance concerns, ensuring data doesn't leave the local network.

- **Resilience:** Edge storage can provide data redundancy and resilience in case of network outages or cloud connectivity issues.

b. Use Cases:

Edge storage is vital in various IoT scenarios, such as:

- **Industrial Automation:** Storing data locally on the factory floor for immediate control and decision-making.

- **Autonomous Vehicles:** Vehicles need to store sensor data locally for real-time navigation and decision-making.

- **Smart Buildings:** Local storage can manage data from sensors and control systems within a building.

3. Fog Data Storage:

a. Significance:

Fog computing, an intermediate layer between edge and cloud, involves storing and processing data on local devices or gateways that are closer to the data source but more powerful than typical edge devices. Fog storage offers benefits such as:

- **Real-Time Processing:** Fog storage enables real-time data processing, analysis, and decision-making at the network edge.

- **Reduced Network Traffic:** By processing and storing data locally, fog computing reduces the amount of data that needs to be sent to the cloud, saving bandwidth.

- **Improved Efficiency:** Fog storage optimizes data handling by filtering and aggregating data at the edge, reducing the cloud's processing burden.

b. Use Cases:

Fog storage is instrumental in applications like:

- **Smart Grids:** Managing and optimizing energy distribution at the edge, reducing network congestion and response time.

- **Healthcare:** Local processing of patient data from medical devices, ensuring immediate responses and privacy compliance.

- **Smart Agriculture:** Aggregating and processing data from multiple sensors in the field for real-time decisions on irrigation, pest control, and crop health.

4. Data Management Strategies:

Organizations adopt various data management strategies in IoT:

- **Data Tiering:** Data is categorized based on its importance, with critical data processed and stored locally (edge/fog) and less critical data sent to the cloud for long-term storage and analysis.

- **Data Synchronization:** Ensuring that data is synchronized between edge, fog, and cloud storage to maintain consistency and reliability.

- **Security and Encryption:** Implementing robust security

measures, including encryption and access controls, to protect stored data from unauthorized access.

Conclusion:

Data storage is a cornerstone of IoT, providing the foundation for data analysis, decision-making, and insights that drive innovation and efficiency. Selecting the right storage strategy—cloud, edge, or fog—depends on the specific requirements of IoT applications, including data volume, latency, privacy, and compliance. By understanding the significance and characteristics of each storage solution, organizations can tailor their IoT deployments to meet their unique needs while unlocking the transformative potential of the connected world.

C. Data Processing and Analytics in IoT: Extracting Value from the Data Deluge

Data processing and analytics are the driving forces behind the transformative potential of the Internet of Things (IoT). In the vast IoT ecosystem, where data is continuously generated by myriad sensors and devices, the ability to process and analyze this data is paramount. It allows organizations to derive actionable insights, make informed decisions, optimize operations, and innovate across various domains. In this exploration, we delve into the world of data processing and analytics in IoT, uncovering their significance, techniques, challenges, and the profound impact they have on shaping the connected world.

1. Significance of Data Processing and Analytics in IoT:

a. Real-Time Insights:

- Data processing and analytics enable real-time monitoring and decision-making, crucial for applications like industrial automation, healthcare, and autonomous vehicles.

b. Predictive Maintenance:

- Analytics can identify patterns and anomalies in sensor data, predicting when equipment or devices are likely to fail, thereby reducing downtime and maintenance costs.

c. Operational Optimization:

- Data-driven insights can optimize processes, such as supply chain management, by providing visibility into bottlenecks and inefficiencies.

d. Improved Customer Experience:

- Analytics can personalize user experiences, such as smart homes adjusting settings based on user preferences or retail stores offering tailored recommendations.

2. Data Processing Techniques:

a. Stream Processing:

- Stream processing technologies like Apache Kafka and Apache Flink analyze data in real time as it's generated, enabling immediate actions based on insights.

b. Batch Processing:

- Batch processing, often used for historical data analysis, involves processing data in predefined chunks or batches, enabling more comprehensive analysis but with some latency.

c. Edge Processing:

- Edge processing involves analyzing data locally on IoT devices or gateways, reducing latency and bandwidth usage. It's suitable for applications requiring real-time responses.

3. Data Analytics Techniques:

a. Descriptive Analytics:

- Descriptive analytics involves summarizing historical data to understand past events and trends, providing the basis for further analysis.

b. Predictive Analytics:

- Predictive analytics uses historical data and machine learning algorithms to forecast future events or trends, such as predicting equipment failures.

c. Prescriptive Analytics:

- Prescriptive analytics takes predictive analytics a step further by recommending actions to optimize outcomes, such as suggesting maintenance schedules.

4. Challenges in Data Processing and Analytics in IoT:

a. Data Volume:

- Handling the sheer volume of data generated by IoT devices, especially in large-scale deployments, can be challenging.

b. Data Variety:

- IoT data can come in various formats, including text, images, and sensor readings, making it complex to process and analyze.

c. Data Quality:

- Ensuring data accuracy and reliability is crucial for meaningful analysis. IoT data can be noisy and may require cleaning.

d. Latency:

- Real-time analytics often require low-latency processing,

which can be challenging in distributed IoT environments.

e. Security and Privacy:

- Analyzing sensitive data in a secure and privacy-compliant manner is essential to prevent data breaches and ensure regulatory compliance.

5. Data Processing and Analytics Tools:

a. Apache Spark:

- Apache Spark is a popular open-source framework for big data processing, offering both batch and stream processing capabilities.

b. Machine Learning Libraries:

- Libraries like TensorFlow and scikit-learn enable machine learning and predictive analytics on IoT data.

c. Cloud-Based Services:

- Cloud providers offer managed services for data processing and analytics, such as AWS Lambda, Google Cloud Dataflow, and Azure Stream Analytics.

d. Edge Analytics Platforms:

- Edge analytics platforms like AWS IoT Greengrass and Microsoft Azure IoT Edge enable local data processing on IoT devices.

6. Use Cases:

a. Smart Manufacturing:

- Predictive maintenance and real-time analytics improve production efficiency and reduce downtime.

b. Healthcare:

- Remote patient monitoring and predictive analytics enhance healthcare outcomes.

c. Agriculture:

- Data analytics optimize irrigation and fertilization, increasing crop yields.

d. Smart Cities:

- Traffic management, waste management, and public safety benefit from real-time analytics.

Conclusion:

Data processing and analytics are the engines that drive IoT's transformative potential, allowing organizations to turn raw data into actionable insights, optimized operations, and innovative solutions. By understanding the significance, techniques, and challenges of data processing and analytics in IoT, organizations can harness the full potential of the connected world, fostering innovation and efficiency across various industries and domains.

D. Real-time and Batch Processing in IoT: Balancing Speed and Scale

In the vast landscape of the Internet of Things (IoT), data processing is the linchpin that translates raw data into actionable insights, driving real-time decision-making and enabling analytics. Two fundamental approaches to data processing in IoT are real-time processing and batch processing. These approaches are tailored to different requirements and use cases, each with its own advantages and challenges. In this exploration, we delve into the intricacies of real-time and batch processing in IoT, uncovering their significance, techniques, and their pivotal role in extracting value from the data deluge.

1. Real-time Processing:

a. Significance:

- Real-time processing, also known as stream processing, involves the analysis of data as it is generated by IoT devices. It offers several advantages:

- **Immediate Action:** Real-time processing enables immediate actions based on insights, making it essential for applications like autonomous vehicles, industrial automation, and remote monitoring.

- **Low Latency:** Real-time processing reduces data latency, ensuring that decisions are made swiftly, which is critical for time-sensitive applications.

- **Continuous Monitoring:** IoT deployments requiring continuous monitoring and immediate response, such as environmental monitoring and security systems, rely on real-time processing.

b. Technologies:

- Real-time processing in IoT utilizes technologies like Apache Kafka, Apache Flink, and Spark Streaming. These frameworks allow data to be analyzed as it flows, enabling instant insights and actions.

c. Use Cases:

- Real-time processing is ideal for various IoT scenarios, including:

- **Autonomous Vehicles:** Vehicles need real-time processing to make split-second decisions based on sensor data.

- **Manufacturing:** Continuous monitoring of equipment for predictive maintenance and quality control.

- **Healthcare:** Immediate alerts for patient monitoring and emergency response.

2. Batch Processing:

a. Significance:

- Batch processing involves the analysis of data in predefined chunks or batches. While it doesn't offer real-time insights, it has its own set of advantages:

- **Comprehensive Analysis:** Batch processing is suitable for historical data analysis, allowing organizations to gain comprehensive insights over longer time periods.

- **Resource Efficiency:** Batch processing can be more resource-efficient for complex analytics tasks that don't require immediate results.

- **Scalability:** Batch processing can handle large volumes of data and can be easily parallelized for high scalability.

b. Technologies:

- Batch processing in IoT relies on technologies like Apache Hadoop and Apache Spark's batch processing capabilities. These frameworks allow data to be ingested, processed, and analyzed in defined intervals.

c. Use Cases:

- Batch processing is instrumental in IoT use cases such as:

- **Big Data Analytics:** Analyzing historical data to identify long-term trends and patterns.

- **Regulatory Compliance:** Archiving data for compliance with regulations that require data retention.

- **Supply Chain Optimization:** Analyzing data in batches to optimize inventory and logistics.

3. Real-time vs. Batch Processing:

a. Latency:

- Real-time processing offers low-latency insights, while batch processing introduces some latency as data must be collected and processed in predefined intervals.

b. Complexity:

- Batch processing can handle complex analytics tasks, while real-time processing is better suited for simpler, immediate actions.

c. Scalability:

- Both real-time and batch processing can be scaled horizontally to handle large volumes of data.

d. Resource Usage:

- Real-time processing may require more resources as data must be processed continuously, while batch processing can be more resource-efficient for certain tasks.

4. Hybrid Approaches:

- Many IoT systems utilize hybrid approaches, combining real-time and batch processing to achieve the benefits of both. For example, real-time processing may be used for immediate alerting and actions, while batch processing is employed for historical data analysis.

Conclusion:

Real-time and batch processing are the twin pillars of data processing in IoT, each serving distinct requirements and use cases. By understanding the significance, techniques, and advantages of both approaches, organizations can tailor their IoT deployments to balance speed and scale, extracting maximum value from the data deluge and shaping the future of connected ecosystems.

E. Data Privacy and Compliance in IoT: Navigating the Regulatory Maze

In the sprawling landscape of the Internet of Things (IoT), data is the currency that fuels innovation, efficiency, and convenience. However, with this data-driven transformation comes the critical responsibility of safeguarding individual privacy and complying with an increasingly complex web of data protection regulations. Data privacy and compliance in IoT are not only ethical imperatives but also legal obligations that organizations must navigate to avoid costly fines, maintain trust, and protect their reputation. In this exploration, we delve into the multifaceted world of data privacy and compliance in IoT, unraveling its significance, regulatory framework, challenges, and strategies for ensuring data protection in the connected world.

1. Significance of Data Privacy and Compliance in IoT:

a. Privacy Protection:

- Data privacy in IoT is paramount to safeguarding the personal information and sensitive data collected by IoT devices, ensuring it is not misused or exposed to unauthorized parties.

b. Legal Obligations:

- Organizations must comply with data protection laws, such as the General Data Protection Regulation (GDPR) in Europe and the California Consumer Privacy Act (CCPA) in the United States, or face severe financial penalties.

c. Trust and Reputation:

- Ensuring data privacy and compliance fosters trust among users and customers, enhancing an organization's reputation and promoting consumer confidence.

2. Regulatory Framework:

a. GDPR:

- The GDPR, applicable in the European Union (EU), sets stringent requirements for data protection, including user consent, data breach notification, and the right to be forgotten.

b. CCPA:

- The CCPA, in California, grants consumers greater control over their personal data, allowing them to opt out of data sharing and request the deletion of their information.

c. HIPAA:

- The Health Insurance Portability and Accountability Act (HIPAA) in the United States regulates the protection of healthcare-related data, including data generated by IoT devices in healthcare.

d. Industry-Specific Regulations:

- Certain industries, such as finance and telecommunications, have their own data protection regulations that apply to IoT deployments in those sectors.

3. Challenges in Data Privacy and Compliance in IoT:

a. Data Volume and Complexity:

- IoT generates vast amounts of diverse data, making it challenging to identify and protect sensitive information.

b. Data Ownership:

- Determining who owns the data generated by IoT devices can be complex, especially in multi-stakeholder environments.

c. Consent Management:

- Obtaining and managing user consent for data collection and processing can be cumbersome, requiring clear and transparent mechanisms.

d. Data Encryption:

- Ensuring end-to-end encryption of data, both in transit and at rest, is vital for protecting data from unauthorized access.

e. Data Retention Policies:

- Establishing data retention policies that comply with regulations while maintaining the usefulness of data can be challenging.

4. Data Privacy Strategies:

a. Data Minimization:

- Collect and process only the data necessary for the intended purpose, reducing the risk of privacy breaches.

b. Security by Design:

- Build security and privacy features into IoT devices and systems from the outset, rather than as an afterthought.

c. User Education:

- Educate users and customers about data privacy and their rights to make informed decisions regarding data sharing and consent.

d. Data Auditing and Monitoring:

- Implement regular audits and real-time monitoring to detect and respond to potential privacy breaches.

e. Data Protection Impact Assessments (DPIAs):

- Conduct DPIAs to assess the impact of data processing activities on privacy and mitigate risks.

5. Compliance Mechanisms:

a. Consent Management Platforms:

- Use consent management platforms to facilitate user consent collection and management.

b. Privacy-Enhancing Technologies (PETs):

- Employ PETs like homomorphic encryption and secure multi-party computation to protect data while allowing for useful analysis.

c. Data Anonymization and Pseudonymization:

- Anonymize or pseudonymize data to reduce its identifiability and protect user privacy.

d. Privacy by Design Frameworks:

- Adhere to privacy by design frameworks that guide the development of privacy-compliant IoT solutions.

Conclusion:

Data privacy and compliance in IoT are essential components of responsible IoT deployments. Organizations must take proactive measures to protect user data, navigate the regulatory maze, and ensure that their IoT solutions respect individual privacy rights. By understanding the significance, regulatory framework, challenges, and strategies involved in data privacy and compliance, organizations can foster trust, maintain compliance, and successfully navigate the evolving landscape of data protection in the connected world.

CHAPTER 5

IoT Platforms and Middleware

IoT, the Internet of Things, is a sprawling ecosystem of interconnected devices, sensors, and systems, generating vast amounts of data. To harness the full potential of this data-driven revolution, organizations rely on IoT platforms and middleware—the central nervous system of IoT. These technologies serve as the backbone that connects, manages, and orchestrates the diverse components of IoT deployments. In this exploration, we delve into the world of IoT platforms and middleware, uncovering their significance, roles, key functionalities, and the transformative power they hold in shaping the connected world. Welcome to the heart and soul of IoT, where data flows, insights emerge, and innovation thrives.

A. IoT Platforms Overview: Orchestrating the Symphony of Connected Devices

IoT platforms serve as the command centers of the Internet of Things (IoT) ecosystem, orchestrating the myriad devices, sensors, data streams, and applications that comprise this interconnected world. These platforms play a pivotal role in simplifying IoT development, enabling efficient data management, and facilitating the integration of IoT solutions into various industries and domains. In this exploration, we delve into the intricacies of IoT platforms, unraveling their significance, components, functionalities, and the transformative potential they hold in shaping the connected future.

1. Significance of IoT Platforms:

a. Streamlining Development:

- IoT platforms abstract the complexity of IoT development, providing tools and services that simplify device management, data processing, and application development.

b. Data Management:

- They enable efficient data ingestion, storage, and analytics, allowing organizations to derive actionable insights from the vast amount of data generated by IoT devices.

c. Interoperability:

- IoT platforms often facilitate interoperability among devices from different manufacturers and technologies, promoting seamless integration.

d. Scalability:

- They empower IoT deployments to scale horizontally, accommodating an ever-growing number of devices and data points.

2. Components of IoT Platforms:

a. Device Management:

- Device management features enable remote provisioning, monitoring, and control of IoT devices. It includes tasks such as device onboarding, firmware updates, and troubleshooting.

b. Connectivity Management:

- Connectivity management allows IoT devices to connect securely to the platform using various communication protocols, including Wi-Fi, cellular, LoRa, and MQTT.

c. Data Ingestion:

- Data ingestion components collect data from devices, transform it into a usable format, and store it for further processing and analysis.

d. Analytics and Processing:

- IoT platforms often include data analytics and processing capabilities, enabling real-time insights, anomaly detection, and predictive analytics.

e. Application Enablement:

- Application enablement tools facilitate the development of

IoT applications, providing APIs, SDKs, and development environments.

f. Integration:

- Integration components allow IoT solutions to connect with other enterprise systems, such as CRM, ERP, and data warehouses.

g. Security and Authentication:

- Security features, including identity management and encryption, ensure the protection of data and devices from cyber threats.

3. Functionalities of IoT Platforms:

a. Device Onboarding:

- Simplifies the process of adding new devices to the IoT network, including provisioning and authentication.

b. Data Processing:

- Enables real-time data processing, including filtering, aggregation, and transformation, to derive actionable insights.

c. Rules and Workflow Engine:

- Provides a mechanism for defining business rules and automating actions based on data and device events.

d. Data Visualization:

- Offers tools to create dashboards and visualizations for monitoring and reporting.

e. Remote Monitoring and Control:

- Allows administrators to remotely monitor device health, update firmware, and control devices.

f. Edge Computing Integration:

- Supports edge computing by deploying IoT platform components at the network edge for low-latency processing.

4. Types of IoT Platforms:

a. Consumer IoT Platforms:

- Designed for smart homes, wearables, and connected consumer devices.

b. Industrial IoT (IIoT) Platforms:

- Tailored for industrial applications, such as manufacturing, predictive maintenance, and supply chain management.

c. Healthcare IoT Platforms:

- Focused on healthcare applications, including remote patient monitoring and medical device management.

d. Agriculture IoT Platforms:

- Optimized for precision agriculture, managing data from sensors in the field.

e. Smart City IoT Platforms:

- Deployed in urban environments to manage smart lighting, waste management, and traffic control systems.

5. Key Players in IoT Platforms:

- Major technology companies, including AWS IoT, Microsoft Azure IoT, and Google Cloud IoT, offer comprehensive IoT platforms. Additionally, there are specialized IoT platform providers catering to specific industries and use cases.

Conclusion:

IoT platforms are the linchpin of IoT deployments, providing the infrastructure and tools necessary to connect, manage, and extract value from the diverse array of IoT devices and data streams. By understanding the significance, components, functionalities, and types of IoT platforms, organizations can harness the full potential of IoT, driving innovation, efficiency, and transformation across various industries and domains.

B. Edge Computing and Fog Computing in IoT: Bringing Intelligence to the Network's Edge

In the ever-evolving landscape of the Internet of Things (IoT), where data is generated at a staggering pace, edge computing and fog computing have emerged as essential paradigms. These distributed computing models bring intelligence closer to the data source—whether on the edge devices themselves or within the local network—empowering IoT deployments with real-time processing, reduced latency, and enhanced efficiency. In this exploration, we delve into the intricacies of edge computing and fog computing in IoT, unveiling their significance, characteristics, use cases, and the transformative potential they hold in shaping the connected world.

1. Edge Computing:

a. Significance of Edge Computing in IoT:

- Edge computing, as the name suggests, pushes computational capabilities to the network's edge, closer to where data is generated. It serves several key purposes in IoT:

- **Low Latency:** Edge computing reduces data transmission latency, making it suitable for applications requiring real-time or near-real-time responses, such as autonomous vehicles and industrial automation.

- **Local Data Processing:** By processing data locally on edge devices or gateways, it minimizes the amount of data sent to central servers, saving bandwidth and cloud computing costs.

- **Resilience:** Edge computing can provide resilience in case of network outages or cloud service interruptions, allowing devices to continue functioning locally.

b. Characteristics of Edge Computing:

- **Local Processing:** Data is processed on the edge device or gateway, closer to the data source.

- **Reduced Bandwidth:** Only relevant data is transmitted to central systems, reducing network traffic.

- **Real-time Responsiveness:** Edge devices can make immediate decisions based on locally processed data.

c. Use Cases for Edge Computing in IoT:

- **Autonomous Vehicles:** Edge computing enables real-time decision-making for navigation and collision avoidance.

- **Industrial Automation:** Edge devices can control manufacturing processes locally for immediate response.

- **Smart Cities:** Traffic management, public safety, and environmental monitoring benefit from edge computing.

2. Fog Computing:

a. Significance of Fog Computing in IoT:

- Fog computing extends the concept of edge computing by introducing an intermediate layer of computing nodes between the edge devices and centralized cloud servers. It plays a critical role in IoT by:

- **Real-time Processing:** Fog computing can process data locally in real-time, offering the benefits of both edge and cloud computing.

- **Data Reduction:** It filters and aggregates data at the edge, reducing the volume of data sent to the cloud and minimizing latency.

- **Edge AI:** Fog computing nodes can support edge AI and machine learning for localized decision-making.

b. Characteristics of Fog Computing:

- **Distributed Nodes:** Fog nodes are distributed throughout the network, providing computational resources close to edge devices.

- **Scalability:** Fog computing can scale horizontally to accommodate more nodes as the network grows.

- **Resource Utilization:** It optimizes resource utilization by offloading computational tasks from edge devices.

c. Use Cases for Fog Computing in IoT:

- **Smart Grids:** Fog computing optimizes energy distribution, reducing network congestion and improving reliability.

- **Healthcare:** Medical data can be processed locally for real-time patient monitoring and immediate interventions.

- **Smart Agriculture:** Data from sensors in the field can be aggregated and processed locally for real-time decision-making on irrigation, pest control, and crop health.

3. Edge vs. Fog Computing:

- Edge computing is focused on processing data as close to the data source as possible, often on the edge device itself or a nearby gateway. Fog computing extends this concept by introducing an intermediate layer of nodes.

- Edge computing is ideal for applications requiring extremely low latency, while fog computing strikes a balance between low latency and cloud computing capabilities.

- Edge computing is suitable for applications like autonomous vehicles and industrial automation, while fog computing is more versatile, accommodating a wider range of use cases.

Conclusion:

Edge computing and fog computing are integral to the IoT ecosystem, bringing intelligence and real-time processing capabilities closer to the data source. By understanding their significance, characteristics, and use cases, organizations can harness the transformative potential of these computing paradigms, driving innovation, efficiency, and responsiveness in an increasingly connected world.

C. IoT Middleware and APIs: Enabling Seamless Communication and Integration

IoT Middleware and APIs serve as the connective tissue in the complex web of IoT devices, applications, and data. These components facilitate the seamless exchange of information, enabling devices and systems to communicate, share data, and integrate with one another. In the multifaceted landscape of the Internet of Things (IoT), middleware and APIs play a pivotal role in simplifying development, promoting interoperability, and driving innovation across industries and domains. In this exploration, we delve into the intricacies of IoT middleware and APIs, unraveling their significance, functionalities, challenges, and the transformative power they hold in shaping the connected world.

1. Significance of IoT Middleware and APIs:

a. Integration Facilitation:

- IoT Middleware and APIs act as the bridge that connects disparate devices, systems, and applications, facilitating seamless communication and data exchange.

b. Abstraction of Complexity:

- They abstract the intricacies of IoT communication protocols, making it easier for developers to build applications that can interact with diverse IoT devices.

c. Interoperability:

- Middleware and APIs promote interoperability, enabling devices from different manufacturers and technologies to work together harmoniously.

d. Scalability:

- They empower IoT solutions to scale horizontally, accommodating an ever-growing number of devices and data sources.

2. IoT Middleware:

a. Types of IoT Middleware:

- **Message-Oriented Middleware (MOM):**

  - MOM systems, like MQTT (Message Queuing Telemetry Transport), facilitate the exchange of messages between devices and applications. They are well-suited for real-time communication in IoT.

- **Data-Oriented Middleware:**

  - Data-Oriented Middleware focuses on the efficient storage and retrieval of data, making it suitable for IoT applications requiring data storage and retrieval.

- **Device Management Middleware:**

  - Device management middleware helps manage IoT devices, including provisioning, authentication, and remote control.

b. Functions of IoT Middleware:

- **Message Routing:** Middleware routes messages between devices and applications, ensuring they reach the right destination.

- **Data Transformation:** It can transform data between

different formats or protocols to facilitate communication between devices with varying capabilities.

- **Security:** Middleware often includes security features, such as authentication and encryption, to protect data and devices.

- **Scalability:** Middleware systems can scale to handle a large number of devices and data streams.

3. IoT APIs:

a. Types of IoT APIs:

- **Device APIs:** These APIs enable applications to interact with IoT devices, allowing developers to read data from sensors or control actuators.

- **Cloud APIs:** Cloud APIs facilitate communication between IoT devices and cloud-based services, such as storage, analytics, and machine learning.

- **Service APIs:** Service APIs provide access to specific IoT-related services, such as geolocation, weather data, or payment processing.

b. Functions of IoT APIs:

- **Data Access:** IoT APIs enable applications to access data generated by devices, making it available for analysis or presentation.

- **Device Control:** APIs allow applications to send commands to IoT devices, enabling remote control and automation.

- **Event Handling:** APIs can handle events triggered by IoT devices, such as sending alerts or triggering actions in response to specific conditions.

4. Challenges in IoT Middleware and APIs:

a. Security: Ensuring the security of data and communication between devices and applications is a paramount challenge.

b. Interoperability: IoT devices often use different communication protocols and data formats, making interoperability a challenge that middleware and APIs must address.

c. Scalability: As IoT deployments grow, middleware and APIs must scale to handle the increasing volume of data and devices.

d. Standardization: The lack of standardized APIs and middleware can hinder interoperability and integration.

e. Real-time Processing: For applications requiring real-time responses, middleware and APIs must support low-latency communication.

5. IoT Middleware and API Providers:

- Major cloud service providers like AWS, Microsoft Azure, and Google Cloud offer IoT middleware and API services. Additionally, there are specialized middleware and API providers catering to various IoT use cases and industries.

Conclusion:

IoT Middleware and APIs are the enablers of seamless communication and integration in the IoT ecosystem. By understanding their significance, types, functions, and the challenges they address, organizations can harness the power of these components to simplify IoT development, promote interoperability, and drive innovation in an increasingly connected world.

D. IoT Device Management Platforms: Orchestrating the Connected World

In the sprawling landscape of the Internet of Things (IoT), managing a multitude of devices efficiently and securely is a monumental task. This is where IoT Device Management Platforms come into play. These platforms serve as the central control and monitoring systems that enable organizations to provision, configure, monitor, update, and troubleshoot IoT devices at scale. In this exploration, we delve into the intricacies of IoT Device Management Platforms, unraveling their significance, key functionalities, challenges, and the pivotal role they play in shaping the connected world.

1. Significance of IoT Device Management Platforms:

a. Device Lifecycle Management:

- Device Management Platforms facilitate the entire device lifecycle, from onboarding and provisioning to retirement, ensuring devices operate effectively throughout their lifespan.

b. Remote Monitoring and Control:

- They enable real-time monitoring, remote diagnostics, and the ability to remotely control and manage devices, reducing the need for physical intervention.

c. Security and Compliance:

- Device Management Platforms enforce security policies, manage device certificates, and ensure compliance with industry regulations, protecting devices and data from vulnerabilities.

d. Scalability:

- These platforms are essential for managing large-scale IoT deployments with thousands or even millions of devices, ensuring consistent performance and updates.

2. Key Functionalities of IoT Device Management Platforms:

a. Device Onboarding and Provisioning:

- Platforms simplify the process of adding new devices to the network, including authenticating and registering devices, assigning identities, and configuring network settings.

b. Configuration Management:

- They enable the remote configuration of devices, allowing changes to device settings, parameters, and firmware updates without physical access.

c. Monitoring and Diagnostics:

- Real-time monitoring and diagnostics tools provide insights into device health, performance, and data quality, helping identify and resolve issues promptly.

d. Firmware and Software Updates:

- Device Management Platforms streamline the deployment of firmware and software updates, ensuring devices are running the latest versions with bug fixes and security patches.

e. Security Management:

- These platforms enforce security policies, manage device

certificates, and support security measures such as device authentication and encryption.

f. Reporting and Analytics:

- Robust reporting and analytics capabilities allow organizations to gain insights into device usage, performance, and trends, aiding in decision-making and optimization.

g. Remote Lock and Wipe:

- In case of security breaches or device loss, platforms can remotely lock or wipe devices to protect sensitive data.

3. Challenges in IoT Device Management Platforms:

a. Heterogeneity: Managing diverse IoT devices with varying hardware, operating systems, and communication protocols presents a challenge.

b. Scalability: Ensuring scalability to handle a growing number of devices without compromising performance is essential.

c. Security: Protecting devices from cyber threats and ensuring secure communication and data storage are paramount concerns.

d. Interoperability: Ensuring that the platform can work seamlessly with devices from different manufacturers and technologies is challenging.

e. Over-the-Air Updates: Managing firmware and software updates, especially in remote or resource-constrained devices, can be complex.

4. Use Cases for IoT Device Management Platforms:

a. Industrial IoT (IIoT):

- Managing sensors, controllers, and machinery in manufacturing and industrial settings for predictive maintenance and operational efficiency.

b. Smart Cities:

- Overseeing devices like smart streetlights, waste management systems, and traffic sensors for optimizing urban infrastructure.

c. Healthcare:

- Managing medical devices, patient monitoring equipment, and wearables for remote patient care and data analytics.

d. Smart Homes:

- Controlling and monitoring IoT devices in residential settings, including smart thermostats, security cameras, and voice-activated assistants.

e. Agriculture:

- Managing sensors in precision agriculture for monitoring soil conditions, weather, and irrigation.

Conclusion:

IoT Device Management Platforms are the backbone of large-scale IoT deployments, ensuring efficient, secure, and scalable device management. By understanding their significance, key functionalities, and the challenges they address, organizations can effectively navigate the complexities of IoT device management, driving innovation and efficiency in the connected world.

E. Integration with Enterprise Systems: Bridging IoT and Business Operations

In the ever-evolving landscape of the Internet of Things (IoT), the seamless integration of IoT data and functionality with enterprise systems is a critical aspect of realizing the full potential of connected devices. Integration ensures that IoT-generated data can be leveraged for informed decision-making, automates processes, and enhances the efficiency and competitiveness of businesses across industries. In this exploration, we delve into the intricacies of integrating IoT with enterprise systems, unraveling its significance, use cases, challenges, and the transformative power it holds in shaping the connected business world.

1. Significance of Integration with Enterprise Systems:

a. Data Utilization:

- Integration allows organizations to harness the wealth of data generated by IoT devices, enabling data-driven insights, predictive analytics, and informed decision-making.

b. Automation and Efficiency:

- By integrating IoT data and functionality with enterprise systems, businesses can automate processes, reduce manual intervention, and improve operational efficiency.

c. Cross-Functional Collaboration:

- Integration fosters collaboration across departments and functions by providing a unified view of data and processes, breaking down data silos.

d. Real-time Insights:

- IoT data integrated with enterprise systems empowers organizations to respond to real-time events and take immediate actions based on data analysis.

2. Use Cases for Integration with Enterprise Systems:

a. Supply Chain Optimization:

- Integration with enterprise resource planning (ERP) systems allows for real-time tracking of shipments, inventory management, and demand forecasting.

b. Predictive Maintenance:

- Integration with maintenance management systems (CMMS) enables predictive maintenance based on IoT sensor data, reducing downtime and maintenance costs.

c. Customer Experience Enhancement:

- Integrating IoT data with customer relationship management (CRM) systems provides insights into customer behavior, allowing for personalized services and product recommendations.

d. Energy Management:

- Integration with energy management systems optimizes energy consumption by monitoring and controlling HVAC systems, lighting, and other energy-intensive equipment.

e. Healthcare:

- IoT integration with electronic health records (EHR) systems enhances patient care by providing real-time monitoring and patient data analysis.

3. Challenges in Integration with Enterprise Systems:

a. Data Integration:

- Handling diverse data formats, protocols, and standards generated by IoT devices and integrating them with existing enterprise data can be complex.

b. Security and Privacy:

- Ensuring the secure transfer and storage of IoT data within enterprise systems is crucial, especially when dealing with sensitive information.

c. Scalability:

- As IoT deployments grow, ensuring that the integration architecture can scale to accommodate increasing data volumes and device counts is a challenge.

d. Legacy Systems:

- Many organizations have legacy systems that may not easily support IoT integration, necessitating upgrades or retrofitting.

e. Standardization:

- The lack of standardized integration protocols for IoT devices can hinder interoperability and integration efforts.

4. Integration Technologies and Approaches:

a. APIs (Application Programming Interfaces):

- APIs enable communication and data exchange between IoT platforms/devices and enterprise systems, offering a standardized approach to integration.

b. Middleware:

- Middleware solutions can facilitate data transformation, routing, and protocol translation between IoT devices and enterprise systems.

c. ESB (Enterprise Service Bus):

- ESBs provide a centralized platform for integrating diverse applications, including IoT, by mediating communication and data flow.

d. Cloud Integration Platforms:

- Cloud-based integration platforms offer scalability and flexibility for connecting IoT data to enterprise systems, often via pre-built connectors.

e. Edge Integration:

- In edge computing scenarios, integration may occur at the edge, allowing for real-time processing and local decision-making before sending data to the cloud or enterprise systems.

5. Future Trends:

- The integration landscape is evolving with the advent of edge computing and 5G connectivity, enabling faster and more responsive integration.

- IoT data analytics and machine learning will play a pivotal role in enhancing the value of integrated data, enabling predictive and prescriptive insights.

Conclusion:

Integration with enterprise systems is the linchpin that enables organizations to extract maximum value from their IoT investments. By understanding its significance, use cases, challenges, and the evolving integration technologies, businesses can unlock the transformative potential of IoT, streamline operations, and gain a competitive edge in the connected business world.

CHAPTER 6

IoT Application Development

IoT Application Development represents the creative and technological convergence of the digital and physical worlds. It's the art and science of crafting innovative applications that harness the power of interconnected devices, sensors, and data to solve real-world problems and enhance our lives. In this fast-evolving landscape, developers are at the forefront of shaping the future of IoT, creating solutions that range from smart homes and intelligent cities to industrial automation and healthcare advancements. In this exploration, we embark on a journey into the realm of IoT Application Development, unveiling its significance, challenges, best practices, and the limitless possibilities it offers in our connected world. Welcome to the gateway of innovation and connectivity where imagination meets technology.

A. Programming Languages for IoT: The Code Behind the Connected World

Programming languages serve as the foundation of software development, and in the Internet of Things (IoT) ecosystem, they play a pivotal role in bringing the connected world to life. IoT devices and applications rely on a diverse set of programming languages, each tailored to specific use cases, hardware constraints, and development requirements. In this exploration, we delve into the intricacies of programming languages for IoT, unraveling their significance, characteristics, popular choices, and the impact they have in shaping the future of connectivity.

1. Significance of Programming Languages in IoT:

a. Device Control: Programming languages enable developers to control IoT devices, read sensor data, and perform actions based on real-time inputs.

b. Data Processing: They are essential for processing and analyzing the vast amount of data generated by IoT devices, extracting actionable insights.

c. Application Development: Programming languages are used to build IoT applications that provide end-users with meaningful interactions and functionalities.

d. Efficiency: The choice of programming language can significantly impact the efficiency and resource utilization of IoT devices, especially those with limited hardware resources.

2. Characteristics of Programming Languages for IoT:

a. Resource Efficiency: Some IoT devices have limited memory and processing power, so languages that are lightweight and efficient, such as C and C++, are often preferred.

b. Real-time Capability: For applications requiring real-time responsiveness, languages like Python, Java, and JavaScript can be used with real-time operating systems (RTOS).

c. Interoperability: Languages that support common communication protocols and data formats facilitate interoperability between devices and systems.

d. Security: Robust programming languages with built-in security features are crucial for protecting IoT devices from vulnerabilities.

3. Popular Programming Languages for IoT:

a. C and C++:

- Known for their efficiency and low-level hardware control, C and C++ are commonly used for programming microcontrollers and resource-constrained devices in IoT.

b. Python:

- Python's simplicity and readability make it a popular choice for rapid IoT application development, data analysis, and prototyping.

c. JavaScript:

- JavaScript, especially in combination with Node.js, is used for building web-based IoT applications, interactive dashboards, and server-side scripting.

d. Java:

- Java is chosen for its platform independence and suitability for building Android-based IoT applications.

e. Rust:

- Rust is gaining popularity for its focus on safety, making it well-suited for IoT devices where security is a primary concern.

f. Go (Golang):

- Go is appreciated for its simplicity, speed, and efficiency, making it a suitable choice for developing IoT applications.

g. Lua:

- Lua's lightweight nature makes it suitable for embedded systems and IoT devices with limited resources.

4. Use Cases and Language Selection:

a. Industrial IoT (IIoT):

- C and C++ are often chosen for controlling industrial sensors and actuators.

b. Consumer IoT (Smart Homes):

- Python and JavaScript are popular for developing user-friendly IoT applications for smart homes.

c. Edge Computing:

- Languages like Rust and Go are preferred for building edge computing applications that require performance and security.

d. Healthcare IoT:

- Java and Python are used for healthcare IoT applications, such as wearable devices and remote patient monitoring.

e. Agricultural IoT:

- Lua is suitable for resource-constrained agricultural IoT devices used in farming.

5. Future Trends:

- As IoT continues to evolve, languages optimized for machine learning and AI, such as TensorFlow (Python), are becoming essential for edge devices.

- Languages that support IoT security features, including secure boot, encryption, and device attestation, will gain prominence.

Conclusion:

Programming languages for IoT are the building blocks that bring connectivity, intelligence, and functionality to the vast array of IoT devices and applications. By understanding their significance, characteristics, and the role they play in IoT use cases, developers and organizations can make informed choices, harness the potential of IoT, and drive innovation in an increasingly connected world.

B. Developing IoT Applications: Bridging the Physical and Digital Realms

IoT (Internet of Things) applications are the dynamic bridge between the physical world of sensors, actuators, and devices and the digital realm of data, analytics, and user interfaces. These applications are the means through which we interact with and make sense of the vast network of interconnected IoT devices. They come in various forms, including embedded, web-based, and mobile applications, each tailored to specific use cases and user needs. In this exploration, we delve into the intricacies of developing IoT applications, unraveling their significance, challenges, development approaches, and the pivotal role they play in shaping the connected world.

1. Significance of IoT Applications:

a. User Interaction: IoT applications serve as the primary interface between users and IoT devices, allowing users to monitor, control, and interact with the physical world.

b. Data Visualization: They provide meaningful data visualizations and insights, making it easier for users to understand the information generated by IoT devices.

c. Automation: IoT applications enable automation and orchestration of actions based on data from sensors and devices, improving efficiency and convenience.

d. Decision Support: These applications assist users and organizations in making informed decisions by presenting actionable data and insights.

2. Types of IoT Applications:

a. Embedded IoT Applications:

- **Characteristics:**

  - Embedded applications run directly on IoT devices or gateways, often with real-time requirements and limited resources.

- **Use Cases:**

  - Embedded applications are used in scenarios where immediate local processing is crucial, such as industrial automation and autonomous vehicles.

b. Web-based IoT Applications:

- **Characteristics:**

  - Web applications are accessed through web browsers on various devices, providing a platform-independent interface for IoT.

- **Use Cases:**

  - Web applications are suitable for monitoring and controlling IoT devices remotely, such as smart home management and energy monitoring.

c. Mobile IoT Applications:

- **Characteristics:**

  - Mobile applications are designed for smartphones and tablets, offering a convenient and portable means of IoT interaction.

- **Use Cases:**

  - Mobile applications are employed in scenarios where

users need on-the-go access to IoT data and control, like fitness trackers and healthcare apps.

3. Challenges in Developing IoT Applications:

a. Heterogeneity: IoT devices vary in terms of hardware, communication protocols, and data formats, making application development complex.

b. Security: Ensuring the security and privacy of IoT data and communication is paramount, especially in applications that handle sensitive information.

c. Scalability: As IoT deployments grow, applications must be scalable to handle an increasing number of devices and data points.

d. Real-time Processing: Some applications require real-time processing and responsiveness, necessitating efficient algorithms and architecture.

e. User Experience: Creating intuitive and user-friendly interfaces is crucial for ensuring the adoption and usability of IoT applications.

4. Development Approaches for IoT Applications:

a. Platform-based Development:

- Some IoT platforms offer development environments and

tools for building applications that integrate seamlessly with the platform's ecosystem.

b. Custom Development:

- Custom development allows for tailored IoT applications designed to meet specific use cases and user requirements.

c. Low-Code/No-Code Development:

- Low-code/no-code platforms simplify IoT application development, allowing users with limited coding skills to create applications through visual interfaces.

5. IoT Application Development Best Practices:

a. Data Handling: Implement efficient data processing and storage techniques to handle the volume and velocity of IoT data.

b. Security: Incorporate robust security measures, including encryption, authentication, and access control, to protect IoT data and communication.

c. User-Centric Design: Prioritize user experience (UX) by creating intuitive interfaces and providing relevant insights.

d. Testing and Validation: Rigorous testing, including real-world scenario testing, is essential to ensure application reliability.

e. Future-proofing: Consider future scalability and

adaptability in application architecture to accommodate growth and changing requirements.

6. Future Trends:

- IoT applications will increasingly leverage edge computing and artificial intelligence for real-time processing and decision-making.

- Interoperability and standardization efforts will simplify the development of cross-platform and cross-device IoT applications.

Conclusion:

IoT applications are the vital link between people and the IoT ecosystem, enabling users to harness the power of connected devices. By understanding their significance, challenges, development approaches, and best practices, developers and organizations can create IoT applications that enhance user experiences, drive efficiency, and pave the way for innovation in the connected world.

C. IoT Application Frameworks: Accelerating Innovation in the Connected World

IoT (Internet of Things) application frameworks are the scaffolding upon which developers build innovative and robust

IoT solutions. These frameworks provide a set of pre-defined tools, libraries, and best practices that streamline the development of IoT applications. They enable developers to focus on creating value-added features and functionalities while abstracting the complexity of working with diverse IoT devices, data, and communication protocols. In this exploration, we delve into the intricacies of IoT application frameworks, unraveling their significance, characteristics, popular choices, and the pivotal role they play in shaping the future of connectivity.

1. Significance of IoT Application Frameworks:

a. Accelerated Development: Frameworks expedite IoT application development by providing reusable components and standardized patterns.

b. Device Agnosticism: They abstract the heterogeneity of IoT devices, enabling developers to work with a wide range of devices seamlessly.

c. Scalability: IoT application frameworks often offer scalability features, allowing applications to grow and adapt to changing needs.

d. Security: Many frameworks incorporate security measures, helping developers implement secure IoT solutions.

2. Characteristics of IoT Application Frameworks:

a. Device Abstraction: Frameworks provide a unified interface to communicate with different types of IoT devices, hiding the complexities of various protocols and hardware.

b. Data Handling: They often include tools for efficiently processing and managing the vast amount of data generated by IoT devices.

c. Connectivity: IoT frameworks offer features for connecting and controlling devices, often supporting both local and cloud-based communication.

d. Analytics and Insights: Some frameworks provide built-in analytics and reporting capabilities for extracting valuable insights from IoT data.

e. Security and Compliance: Security features such as encryption, authentication, and compliance with industry standards are often included.

3. Popular IoT Application Frameworks:

a. **Arduino IoT Cloud:** Arduino's cloud-based platform offers an IoT development framework for building connected applications using Arduino devices.

b. **AWS IoT Core:** Amazon Web Services (AWS) provides a

comprehensive IoT application framework, including device management, data processing, and analytics.

c. **Google Cloud IoT:** Google's IoT framework integrates with Google Cloud services, offering tools for device management, data analysis, and machine learning.

d. **Microsoft Azure IoT:** Azure IoT provides a robust framework for developing, deploying, and managing IoT applications, including support for edge computing.

e. **IBM Watson IoT:** IBM's IoT platform includes a framework for building IoT applications that leverage AI and machine learning for data analysis.

f. **Particle IoT:** Particle offers an IoT development platform with hardware and software components, facilitating rapid prototyping and deployment.

4. Use Cases for IoT Application Frameworks:

a. Industrial IoT (IIoT):

- Frameworks like AWS IoT and Azure IoT are commonly used to build IIoT applications for predictive maintenance, asset tracking, and process optimization.

b. Smart Cities:

- IoT application frameworks support solutions for smart traffic management, waste management, and environmental monitoring.

c. Healthcare:

- In healthcare, IoT frameworks are used to develop remote patient monitoring and telehealth applications.

d. Smart Homes:

- Frameworks such as Arduino IoT Cloud and Particle IoT enable the development of home automation and smart security systems.

5. Challenges in IoT Application Frameworks:

a. Integration Complexity: Integrating IoT frameworks with existing enterprise systems can be challenging.

b. Learning Curve: Developers may need to learn the specifics of a particular framework, which can vary in complexity.

c. Vendor Lock-in: Some frameworks are tied to specific cloud providers, potentially leading to vendor lock-in.

d. Customization: While frameworks provide pre-built components, customizing applications for unique use cases may require additional effort.

6. Future Trends:

- IoT application frameworks are likely to evolve to accommodate edge computing, enabling real-time processing at the edge of the network.

- Interoperability standards and open-source frameworks may become more prevalent to foster greater flexibility and avoid vendor lock-in.

Conclusion:

IoT application frameworks are the enablers of rapid and efficient IoT solution development. By understanding their significance, characteristics, popular choices, and the challenges they address, developers and organizations can leverage these frameworks to accelerate innovation, reduce development effort, and pave the way for a connected and data-driven future.

D. Testing and Debugging IoT Solutions: Ensuring Reliability in the Connected World

Testing and debugging are critical phases in the development of Internet of Things (IoT) solutions, ensuring that IoT devices and applications operate reliably in the connected world. The complexity of IoT ecosystems, with diverse hardware, communication protocols, and real-time requirements, makes testing and debugging even more crucial. In this exploration, we delve into the intricacies of testing and debugging IoT solutions, unraveling their significance, challenges, best practices, and the pivotal role they play in ensuring the functionality and security of connected devices and applications.

1. Significance of Testing and Debugging in IoT:

a. Reliability: Testing verifies that IoT devices and applications work as intended, reducing the risk of failures in real-world scenarios.

b. Security: Rigorous testing helps identify vulnerabilities and weaknesses in IoT systems, safeguarding against security breaches.

c. Compliance: IoT solutions often need to adhere to industry standards and regulations, which require thorough testing to demonstrate compliance.

d. User Experience: Effective testing ensures a smooth and user-friendly experience for IoT device users.

2. Challenges in Testing and Debugging IoT Solutions:

a. Heterogeneity: IoT ecosystems consist of diverse devices with varying hardware, communication protocols, and data formats, making testing complex.

b. Scalability: As IoT deployments grow, testing needs to accommodate a large number of devices and data streams.

c. Real-time Requirements: Some IoT applications have stringent real-time requirements, requiring specialized testing methodologies.

d. Edge and Cloud Interactions: IoT solutions often involve data processing both at the edge and in the cloud, necessitating end-to-end testing.

3. Types of Testing for IoT Solutions:

a. Functional Testing: Ensures that IoT devices and applications perform their intended functions correctly.

- **Unit Testing:** Tests individual components or functions within IoT devices or applications.

- **Integration Testing:** Tests the interaction between different components or devices in the IoT ecosystem.

- **End-to-End Testing:** Validates the entire IoT solution, including data flow from devices to the cloud and back.

b. Performance Testing: Evaluates the performance and scalability of IoT systems.

- **Load Testing:** Measures how well the system handles increasing loads of data or device connections.

- **Latency Testing:** Examines response times and latency in data transmission.

- **Stress Testing:** Pushes the system to its limits to identify potential failure points.

c. Security Testing: Identifies vulnerabilities and weaknesses in IoT solutions.

- **Penetration Testing:** Simulates cyberattacks to uncover security flaws.

- **Vulnerability Scanning:** Scans for known security vulnerabilities in IoT devices and software.

- **Security Auditing:** Reviews the security measures implemented in IoT solutions against industry standards.

d. Usability Testing: Assesses the user experience and interface design of IoT applications.

- **User Acceptance Testing (UAT):** Involves real users testing the application to provide feedback on its usability.

4. Debugging IoT Solutions:

a. Remote Debugging: Debugging IoT devices remotely is crucial, as many devices may be located in remote or inaccessible locations. Tools like remote log access and debugging interfaces are essential.

b. Edge Debugging: Debugging at the edge, where real-time processing occurs, often requires specialized tools and techniques to diagnose and fix issues quickly.

c. Simulation and Emulation: Simulating or emulating IoT environments can aid in replicating real-world conditions for testing and debugging.

d. Logging and Monitoring: Implementing comprehensive logging and monitoring systems helps capture and analyze data for debugging purposes.

5. Best Practices:

a. Test Early and Often: Start testing IoT solutions as early as possible in the development process and continue testing throughout the project.

b. Real-world Testing: Whenever possible, conduct testing in conditions that mimic real-world usage scenarios.

c. Data Security: Ensure that sensitive data is protected during testing, especially when using real data.

d. Automation: Implement test automation to streamline repetitive and time-consuming testing tasks.

e. Collaboration: Promote collaboration among developers, testers, and other stakeholders to identify and address issues effectively.

6. Future Trends:

- As IoT evolves, testing and debugging tools and techniques will continue to adapt to handle the growing complexity and scale of IoT ecosystems.

- AI and machine learning may play a more significant role in automating testing and identifying anomalies in IoT solutions.

Conclusion:

Testing and debugging are the cornerstones of ensuring the reliability, security, and functionality of IoT solutions. By understanding their significance, challenges, types, and best practices, developers and organizations can navigate the complexities of IoT testing, build robust solutions, and provide users with a seamless and secure connected experience.

E. Continuous Integration/Continuous Deployment (CI/CD) in IoT: Driving Efficiency and Quality in Connected Systems

Continuous Integration/Continuous Deployment (CI/CD) practices have transformed software development by automating the building, testing, and deployment of applications. In the context of the Internet of Things (IoT), where diverse devices and complex ecosystems are the norm, CI/CD becomes even more crucial. CI/CD pipelines ensure that IoT systems and applications are developed, tested, and deployed efficiently, enhancing the quality, reliability, and agility of IoT solutions. In this exploration, we delve into the intricacies of CI/CD in IoT, unraveling its significance, challenges, best practices, and the transformative impact it has on the connected world.

1. Significance of CI/CD in IoT:

a. Speed and Efficiency: CI/CD automates repetitive tasks, enabling rapid development and deployment of IoT solutions.

b. Quality Assurance: Continuous testing ensures that IoT applications and devices meet quality standards, reducing the risk of errors in production.

c. Scalability: CI/CD pipelines can scale to accommodate the growing complexity and scale of IoT ecosystems.

d. Risk Reduction: Automated testing and deployment reduce the likelihood of critical failures in IoT systems.

2. Challenges in CI/CD for IoT:

a. Device Heterogeneity: IoT systems often involve a wide range of devices with varying hardware, software, and communication protocols, complicating testing and deployment.

b. Real-time Processing: Some IoT applications require real-time data processing and responsiveness, necessitating specialized CI/CD approaches.

c. Edge Computing: CI/CD pipelines need to support edge computing, where processing occurs at the device level, not just in the cloud.

d. Connectivity Issues: IoT devices may operate in remote or unreliable network environments, affecting CI/CD processes.

3. CI/CD Components for IoT:

a. Source Control: Manage code repositories to track changes, version control, and collaboration among developers.

b. Build Automation: Automate the compilation, packaging, and deployment of IoT applications and firmware.

c. Testing Automation: Automate the testing of IoT devices, including functional, performance, and security testing.

d. Continuous Deployment: Automatically deploy IoT applications to production environments, including edge devices and cloud services.

e. Monitoring and Feedback: Implement monitoring systems to gather data on IoT systems' performance in real-time and provide feedback to developers.

4. CI/CD Best Practices for IoT:

a. Containerization: Use containerization technologies like Docker to package IoT applications and their dependencies for consistent deployment across environments.

b. Automated Testing: Implement automated testing frameworks that cover a range of test cases, including device compatibility, scalability, and security.

c. Infrastructure as Code (IaC): Use IaC tools like Terraform or Ansible to automate the provisioning of IoT infrastructure.

d. Continuous Monitoring: Monitor IoT systems and devices in production to detect issues and vulnerabilities in real-time.

e. Version Control: Maintain comprehensive version control for IoT device firmware and application code.

5. CI/CD in Edge Computing:

a. Edge CI/CD: Implement CI/CD pipelines that include edge devices, ensuring that edge computing applications are tested and deployed efficiently.

b. Over-the-Air (OTA) Updates: Enable OTA updates for IoT devices to facilitate seamless updates and patches in the field.

6. Future Trends:

- As IoT continues to evolve, CI/CD practices will adapt to accommodate edge computing and real-time processing requirements.

- AI and machine learning will play a significant role in automating testing and deployment decisions based on data analytics.

Conclusion:

CI/CD practices have become indispensable in the development and deployment of IoT solutions. By understanding their significance, addressing challenges, and implementing best practices, developers and organizations can harness the power of CI/CD to streamline IoT development, enhance quality, and ensure the reliability and agility of connected systems in an ever-evolving IoT landscape.

CHAPTER 7

IoT Security

The rapid proliferation of the Internet of Things (IoT) has ushered in a new era of connectivity, transforming the way we live, work, and interact with the world around us. While IoT offers unprecedented opportunities for innovation and convenience, it also introduces a host of security challenges and vulnerabilities. IoT Security is the linchpin that ensures the integrity, confidentiality, and availability of data in this hyper-connected ecosystem. In this exploration, we delve into the intricate world of IoT security, unraveling its significance, complexities, threats, best practices, and the critical role it plays in safeguarding our connected future. Welcome to the realm where technology meets security, and where the connected world is fortified against digital threats.

A. Security in IoT Devices: Safeguarding the Foundation of Connectivity

IoT devices are the foundation of the Internet of Things ecosystem, collecting data, performing actions, and enabling the interconnected world we live in. However, they are also the most vulnerable components, prone to various security threats due to their distributed nature, resource constraints, and diverse use cases. Ensuring the security of IoT devices is paramount to protect against data breaches, cyberattacks, and the compromise of critical infrastructure. In this exploration, we delve into the intricacies of security in IoT devices, unraveling its significance, challenges, best practices, and the vital role it plays in fortifying the backbone of connectivity.

1. Significance of Security in IoT Devices:

a. Data Protection: IoT devices handle sensitive data, including personal information and operational data, which must be safeguarded against unauthorized access.

b. Critical Infrastructure: Many IoT devices are integrated into critical infrastructure, such as healthcare, energy, and transportation systems, where security breaches can have severe consequences.

c. Reputation and Trust: Security breaches in IoT devices can erode trust in the technology, impacting user adoption and market success.

d. Regulatory Compliance: Many industries and regions have stringent regulations governing data security and privacy, necessitating security measures in IoT devices.

2. Challenges in IoT Device Security:

a. Resource Constraints: IoT devices often have limited processing power, memory, and storage, making it challenging to implement robust security measures.

b. Diversity: The vast array of IoT devices, each with different hardware, software, and communication protocols, presents a challenge for standardization and uniform security practices.

c. Lifespan: IoT devices may have long lifespans, and ensuring security throughout their operational lifecycle is a complex task.

d. Remote Management: Many IoT devices are deployed in remote or inaccessible locations, making updates and security patches challenging.

3. Key Aspects of IoT Device Security:

a. Authentication and Authorization: Implement strong authentication mechanisms to ensure that only authorized users and devices can access IoT devices and data.

b. Data Encryption: Encrypt data both in transit and at rest to protect it from eavesdropping and tampering.

c. Secure Boot and Firmware Updates: Ensure that IoT devices boot securely and can receive and apply firmware updates securely.

d. Access Control: Enforce access control policies to limit access to IoT devices and data to authorized entities.

e. Device Identity and Management: Assign unique identities to each IoT device and manage these identities throughout their lifecycle.

f. Secure Communication: Implement secure communication protocols, such as TLS/SSL, to protect data in transit.

4. Best Practices for IoT Device Security:

a. Security by Design: Integrate security into the design and development process of IoT devices, rather than treating it as an afterthought.

b. Regular Patching and Updates: Provide mechanisms for regular updates and patches to address security vulnerabilities.

c. Network Segmentation: Segment IoT devices from critical networks to minimize the potential impact of a breach.

d. Monitoring and Anomaly Detection: Implement continuous monitoring and anomaly detection to identify and respond to security threats in real-time.

e. Security Auditing: Regularly audit IoT devices and systems for security vulnerabilities and compliance with security policies.

5. Emerging Technologies for IoT Device Security:

- **Blockchain:** Provides decentralized and tamper-resistant transaction records, enhancing the integrity of data.

- **Hardware Security Modules (HSMs):** Secure hardware elements that provide cryptographic key management and protection.

- **Zero Trust Architecture:** A security model that assumes no trust within the network and verifies identity and security at every interaction.

6. Future Trends:

- As IoT continues to grow, security standards and regulations are likely to become more stringent, driving the adoption of stronger security practices.

- The integration of AI and machine learning will play a role in anomaly detection and threat mitigation in IoT devices.

Conclusion:

Security in IoT devices is the bedrock upon which the trust and reliability of the entire IoT ecosystem are built. By understanding its significance, challenges, best practices, and the role of emerging technologies, device manufacturers and organizations can fortify the security of IoT devices, mitigating risks and ensuring the continued growth and success of IoT in our interconnected world.

B. Secure Communication in IoT: Building Trust in a Connected World

Secure communication is the cornerstone of trust in the Internet of Things (IoT) ecosystem, where billions of devices transmit sensitive data across diverse networks. Protecting data from eavesdropping, tampering, and unauthorized access is paramount in ensuring the integrity and privacy of IoT systems. Secure communication protocols, encryption, and authentication mechanisms play a pivotal role in safeguarding data in transit and building trust among users and organizations. In this exploration, we delve into the intricacies of secure communication in IoT, unraveling its significance, challenges, best practices, and the critical role it plays in fortifying the foundation of trust in our connected world.

1. Significance of Secure Communication in IoT:

a. Data Privacy: Secure communication ensures that sensitive data, such as personal information and industrial data, remains confidential and protected.

b. Data Integrity: It safeguards data from unauthorized tampering, ensuring that data received is the same as what was sent.

c. Authentication: Secure communication verifies the identities of devices and entities, preventing unauthorized access.

d. Regulatory Compliance: Many industries and regions have stringent regulations governing data privacy and security, mandating secure communication practices.

2. Challenges in Secure Communication in IoT:

a. Heterogeneity: IoT devices use a wide range of communication protocols and hardware, requiring flexible security solutions.

b. Resource Constraints: Many IoT devices have limited processing power, memory, and energy, making it challenging to implement robust encryption and authentication.

c. Scale: IoT ecosystems involve a massive number of devices, each requiring secure communication, which can strain network resources.

d. Real-time Requirements: Some IoT applications require real-time data transmission, necessitating efficient secure communication protocols.

3. Key Components of Secure Communication in IoT:

a. Encryption: Encrypt data to protect it from unauthorized access, ensuring that even if intercepted, the data remains unreadable.

b. Authentication: Verify the identities of devices and entities to prevent unauthorized access to IoT systems.

c. Integrity Checks: Implement mechanisms to verify that data hasn't been tampered with during transmission.

d. Key Management: Securely manage cryptographic keys used for encryption and decryption.

e. Secure Protocols: Utilize communication protocols that support encryption and authentication, such as HTTPS, MQTT-TLS, and CoAP-DTLS.

4. Best Practices for Secure Communication in IoT:

a. Security by Design: Incorporate security into the design and development of IoT devices and communication protocols from the outset.

b. Device Identity: Assign unique identities to each IoT device and authenticate them during communication.

c. Regular Updates: Keep devices and communication protocols up to date with security patches and updates.

d. Minimal Data Exposure: Limit the amount of data exposed to the network and ensure only necessary data is transmitted.

e. Secure Key Management: Use hardware security modules (HSMs) or secure elements for key storage and management.

5. Emerging Technologies for Secure Communication in IoT:

- **Quantum-Safe Cryptography:** Preparing for the future threat of quantum computing, which can break current encryption algorithms.

- **Blockchain:** Provides tamper-resistant transaction records and can be used to enhance trust in data exchange.

6. Future Trends:

- The integration of artificial intelligence and machine learning for anomaly detection and threat mitigation in real-time.

- Increased emphasis on standardization and interoperability in secure communication protocols to simplify IoT security.

Conclusion:

Secure communication is the linchpin that underpins trust and reliability in the IoT ecosystem. By understanding its significance, addressing challenges, and implementing best practices and emerging technologies, device manufacturers and organizations can fortify the security of IoT communication, mitigating risks and ensuring that users can trust the data and interactions within our connected world.

C. Data Encryption and Authentication in IoT: Protecting the Digital Soul of Connected Devices

In the Internet of Things (IoT) landscape, data encryption and authentication are the twin pillars of cybersecurity, safeguarding the digital soul of connected devices. With billions of devices communicating sensitive data across diverse networks, ensuring the confidentiality, integrity, and authenticity of data is paramount. Encryption secures data from unauthorized access, while authentication verifies the identity of devices and entities, preventing malicious actors from infiltrating IoT systems. In this exploration, we delve into the intricacies of data encryption and authentication in IoT, unraveling their significance, techniques, challenges, best practices, and the pivotal role they play in fortifying the security of our interconnected world.

1. Significance of Data Encryption and Authentication in IoT:

a. Data Privacy: Encryption ensures that sensitive data, such as personal information, financial data, and industrial secrets, remains confidential and protected from eavesdropping.

b. Data Integrity: Authentication and encryption collectively safeguard data from unauthorized tampering, ensuring that data received is the same as what was sent.

c. Device and Entity Verification: Authentication verifies the identities of devices and entities, preventing unauthorized access and enhancing trust in data sources.

d. Regulatory Compliance: Compliance with data privacy regulations, such as GDPR, HIPAA, and industry-specific standards, mandates the use of encryption and authentication in IoT systems.

2. Challenges in Data Encryption and Authentication in IoT:

a. Resource Constraints: Many IoT devices have limited processing power, memory, and energy, making it challenging to implement robust encryption and authentication.

b. Heterogeneity: IoT ecosystems encompass a wide range of devices, each with different hardware, software, and communication protocols, requiring flexible security solutions.

c. Scale: IoT ecosystems involve a massive number of devices, each requiring encryption and authentication, which can strain network resources.

d. Real-time Requirements: Some IoT applications require real-time data transmission, necessitating efficient encryption and authentication protocols.

3. Data Encryption in IoT:

a. Symmetric Encryption: Uses the same key for both encryption and decryption and is suitable for resource-constrained IoT devices.

b. Asymmetric Encryption: Utilizes a pair of public and private keys for encryption and decryption, providing enhanced security but requiring more resources.

c. End-to-End Encryption: Encrypts data at the source device and decrypts it only at the intended recipient, ensuring data privacy throughout its journey.

d. Transport Layer Security (TLS): A widely used protocol that ensures secure communication between IoT devices and servers by encrypting data during transit.

4. Authentication in IoT:

a. Device Identity: Assigns unique identities or certificates to each IoT device, ensuring their authenticity during communication.

b. Public Key Infrastructure (PKI): Utilizes digital certificates and a certificate authority (CA) to verify the authenticity of devices and entities.

c. Secure Boot: Ensures that IoT devices boot securely and are not tampered with before operation.

d. Multi-Factor Authentication (MFA): Requires multiple forms of authentication, such as a password and a fingerprint, to enhance security.

5. Best Practices for Data Encryption and Authentication in IoT:

a. Security by Design: Integrate encryption and authentication into the design and development of IoT devices and communication protocols from the outset.

b. Regular Updates: Keep devices, encryption algorithms, and authentication mechanisms up to date with security patches and updates.

c. Minimal Data Exposure: Limit the amount of data exposed to the network and ensure only necessary data is encrypted and authenticated.

d. Secure Key Management: Use hardware security modules (HSMs) or secure elements for key storage and management.

6. Emerging Technologies for Data Encryption and Authentication in IoT:

- **Homomorphic Encryption:** Allows computation on

encrypted data, preserving data privacy during processing.

- **Blockchain:** Provides tamper-resistant transaction records and can be used to enhance trust in data exchange.

7. Future Trends:

- The integration of artificial intelligence and machine learning for anomaly detection and threat mitigation in real-time.

- Increased emphasis on standardization and interoperability in encryption and authentication protocols to simplify IoT security.

Conclusion:

Data encryption and authentication are the guardians of trust and security in the IoT realm. By understanding their significance, addressing challenges, and implementing best practices and emerging technologies, device manufacturers and organizations can fortify the security of IoT data and communication, mitigating risks and ensuring the confidentiality, integrity, and authenticity of data within our interconnected world.

D. Security Best Practices in IoT: Fortifying the Digital Frontier

Security is the bedrock upon which the trust and reliability of the Internet of Things (IoT) ecosystem are built. As IoT continues to permeate every aspect of our lives, from smart homes to critical infrastructure, it becomes increasingly critical to implement robust security practices. Security best practices in IoT encompass a comprehensive approach to safeguarding devices, networks, and data from a myriad of threats. In this exploration, we delve into the intricacies of security best practices in IoT, unraveling their significance, key principles, challenges, and the pivotal role they play in fortifying the digital frontier.

1. Significance of Security Best Practices in IoT:

a. Data Protection: Ensuring the confidentiality and integrity of data is paramount to safeguard sensitive information from theft and tampering.

b. Device Security: Protecting IoT devices from unauthorized access and exploitation prevents potential attacks on the entire ecosystem.

c. Trust and Reliability: Implementing strong security practices fosters trust among users and organizations, ensuring that IoT systems perform reliably.

d. Regulatory Compliance: Many industries and regions have stringent regulations governing data privacy and security, necessitating adherence to security best practices.

2. Key Principles of Security Best Practices in IoT:

a. Defense in Depth: Implement multiple layers of security controls to protect against a wide range of threats. This includes securing devices, networks, and applications.

b. Risk Assessment: Continuously assess and mitigate security risks to adapt to evolving threats.

c. Least Privilege: Restrict access to resources to the minimum necessary for users and devices to perform their functions.

d. Data Encryption and Authentication: Encrypt data and implement authentication mechanisms to protect data in transit and at rest.

e. Regular Updates and Patch Management: Keep devices and software up to date with security patches to address vulnerabilities.

f. Secure Boot and Firmware Validation: Ensure that IoT devices boot securely and validate firmware integrity to prevent tampering.

3. Challenges in Implementing Security Best Practices in IoT:

a. Resource Constraints: Many IoT devices have limited processing power, memory, and storage, making it challenging to implement robust security measures.

b. Heterogeneity: The wide array of IoT devices with varying hardware, software, and communication protocols complicates standardization and uniform security practices.

c. Scale: IoT ecosystems involve a massive number of devices, each requiring security measures, which can strain network resources.

d. Real-time Requirements: Some IoT applications require real-time data transmission, necessitating efficient security protocols.

4. Security Best Practices for IoT:

a. Security by Design: Integrate security into the design and development process of IoT devices, networks, and applications.

b. Secure Device Identity: Assign unique identities or certificates to each IoT device to verify their authenticity.

c. Encryption and Authentication: Implement encryption and authentication mechanisms to protect data and verify identities.

d. Network Segmentation: Segment IoT devices from critical networks to minimize the potential impact of a breach.

e. Continuous Monitoring and Anomaly Detection: Implement continuous monitoring to identify and respond to security threats in real-time.

f. Incident Response Plan: Develop and regularly update an incident response plan to mitigate the impact of security incidents.

5. Emerging Technologies for Security in IoT:

- **Homomorphic Encryption:** Allows computation on encrypted data, preserving data privacy during processing.

- **Blockchain:** Provides tamper-resistant transaction records and can be used to enhance trust in data exchange.

6. Future Trends:

- The integration of artificial intelligence and machine learning for anomaly detection and threat mitigation in real-time.

- Increased emphasis on standardization and interoperability in security protocols to simplify IoT security.

Conclusion:

Security best practices are the foundation of trust and reliability in the IoT realm. By understanding their significance, addressing challenges, and implementing these principles and emerging technologies, device manufacturers and organizations can fortify the security of IoT ecosystems, mitigating risks and ensuring the continued growth and success of IoT in our interconnected world.

E. IoT Security Standards and Regulations: Safeguarding the Connected World

IoT (Internet of Things) security standards and regulations serve as the guiding principles and legal frameworks that govern the development, deployment, and operation of connected devices and systems. In an increasingly interconnected world, where billions of devices transmit sensitive data, ensuring security and privacy is paramount. IoT security standards and regulations are designed to protect against threats, enforce best practices, and mitigate risks. In this exploration, we delve into the intricacies of IoT security standards and regulations, unraveling their significance, key standards, regulatory bodies, challenges, and their pivotal role in safeguarding the connected world.

1. Significance of IoT Security Standards and Regulations:

a. Consumer Trust: Establishing robust security standards instills trust in IoT devices and applications, encouraging their adoption.

b. Interoperability: Standardization promotes compatibility and interoperability among devices, facilitating seamless integration and communication.

c. Data Privacy: Regulations protect the privacy of user data, ensuring that sensitive information is handled responsibly.

d. Cybersecurity: Standards and regulations mitigate cybersecurity risks, reducing the potential for cyberattacks and data breaches.

2. Key IoT Security Standards:

a. ISO/IEC 27001: A widely recognized international standard for information security management systems (ISMS).

b. NIST Cybersecurity Framework: Developed by the National Institute of Standards and Technology (NIST) in the U.S., it provides guidelines and best practices for improving cybersecurity.

c. IEC 62443: A set of standards for industrial automation and control systems (IACS) security.

d. ENISA IoT Baseline Security Recommendations: Published by the European Union Agency for Cybersecurity (ENISA), this provides security recommendations for IoT.

e. OWASP IoT Top Ten: Published by the Open Web Application Security Project (OWASP), it outlines the top security concerns in IoT.

f. IEEE 802.1X: A standard for network access control, which can be applied to secure IoT device access to networks.

3. Regulatory Bodies and Initiatives:

a. GDPR (General Data Protection Regulation): The European Union's regulation that protects the privacy and personal data of individuals.

b. HIPAA (Health Insurance Portability and Accountability Act): In the U.S., HIPAA sets standards for the protection of patient health information, including data from IoT medical devices.

c. FCC (Federal Communications Commission): In the U.S., the FCC regulates IoT devices that use radio frequencies.

d. IoT Cybersecurity Improvement Act: A U.S. law that sets security standards for IoT devices used by federal agencies.

4. Challenges in IoT Security Standards and Regulations:

a. Rapid Technological Evolution: IoT is an ever-evolving field, and standards and regulations must keep pace with new developments.

b. Heterogeneity: IoT encompasses a wide range of devices, each with different capabilities and security needs, making standardization challenging.

c. Global Variations: Different regions and countries may have varying regulations, leading to complexities for multinational IoT deployments.

d. Enforcement: Enforcing regulations and standards across a vast and diverse IoT landscape can be challenging.

5. Compliance and Implementation:

a. Compliance Frameworks: Organizations should establish frameworks to ensure compliance with relevant standards and regulations.

b. Risk Assessment: Conduct regular risk assessments to identify and address security vulnerabilities.

c. Data Protection Impact Assessments: Evaluate the impact of data processing activities on data subjects' privacy and security.

d. Secure Development: Implement security by design principles in IoT device and application development.

6. Future Trends:

- Increasing convergence of international standards to simplify compliance for global IoT deployments.

- Emphasis on secure IoT supply chains, from device manufacturing to deployment.

Conclusion:

IoT security standards and regulations are the guardians of trust and reliability in the interconnected world. By understanding their significance, addressing challenges, and ensuring compliance and implementation, device manufacturers, organizations, and governments can work together to fortify the security and privacy of IoT ecosystems, mitigating risks and ensuring the responsible growth and success of IoT technologies in our digitally connected world.

CHAPTER 8

IoT Protocols

In the vast and intricate realm of the Internet of Things (IoT), where billions of devices seamlessly communicate and collaborate, IoT protocols serve as the universal language that enables this digital symphony. These protocols dictate how devices share data, interact, and ensure the reliability and efficiency of the IoT ecosystem. Whether it's a smart home thermostat, a fleet of industrial sensors, or a wearable fitness tracker, IoT protocols are the essential framework that orchestrates the harmonious exchange of information. In this exploration, we venture into the intricate world of IoT protocols, unraveling their significance, key categories, popular protocols, and the vital role they play in facilitating the connected devices that define our modern world. Welcome to the language of the IoT, where devices converse and data flows seamlessly.

A. MQTT (Message Queuing Telemetry Transport) and CoAP (Constrained Application Protocol): Enabling Efficient Communication in IoT

MQTT and CoAP are two prominent communication protocols

that play a crucial role in the Internet of Things (IoT) by facilitating efficient and lightweight data exchange between connected devices. These protocols are designed to address the unique challenges posed by IoT, such as resource constraints, low bandwidth, and intermittent connectivity. In this exploration, we delve into the intricacies of MQTT and CoAP, unraveling their significance, key features, use cases, and how they contribute to the seamless communication that powers the IoT ecosystem.

MQTT (Message Queuing Telemetry Transport):

1. Significance of MQTT in IoT:

MQTT is a widely adopted publish-subscribe messaging protocol that excels in scenarios where low power consumption, minimal bandwidth usage, and reliable messaging are critical. It is designed for resource-constrained devices and is widely used in various IoT applications, including home automation, industrial monitoring, and telemetry systems.

2. Key Features of MQTT:

a. Publish-Subscribe Model: MQTT operates on a publish-subscribe paradigm, allowing devices to publish data to specific topics and subscribe to topics of interest. This decoupled communication model enhances flexibility and scalability.

b. Quality of Service (QoS): MQTT offers three levels of QoS to ensure message delivery reliability: 0 (At most once), 1 (At least once), and 2 (Exactly once).

c. Retained Messages: MQTT supports retained messages, allowing the last published message on a topic to be retained by the broker and delivered to new subscribers.

d. Last Will and Testament: Devices can specify a "Last Will" message that the broker sends to a specified topic if the device unexpectedly disconnects.

e. Lightweight Protocol: MQTT is designed to be lightweight, making it suitable for resource-constrained IoT devices with limited processing power and memory.

f. Wide Adoption: MQTT has a large and active community, ensuring a wide range of libraries, implementations, and support.

3. Use Cases for MQTT:

- **Smart Homes:** MQTT is commonly used in home automation systems to control and monitor smart devices, such as lights, thermostats, and security cameras.

- **Industrial IoT (IIoT):** In industrial settings, MQTT is used for real-time monitoring and control of machines and processes.

- **Telemetry and Remote Sensing:** MQTT is ideal for

collecting data from sensors and transmitting it to centralized servers for analysis.

CoAP (Constrained Application Protocol):

1. Significance of CoAP in IoT:

CoAP is a lightweight and efficient protocol designed specifically for IoT devices with constrained resources. It is inspired by HTTP but optimized for constrained environments, making it well-suited for IoT applications like sensor networks, smart grids, and wearable devices.

2. Key Features of CoAP:

a. RESTful Communication: CoAP follows a RESTful communication model, which aligns with the design principles of the web and simplifies interaction with IoT resources.

b. Datagram Transport: CoAP operates over the User Datagram Protocol (UDP), minimizing overhead and reducing latency.

c. Resource Discovery: CoAP supports resource discovery, allowing clients to query devices for available resources and their characteristics.

d. Caching: CoAP supports caching of responses to reduce network traffic and improve efficiency.

e. Lightweight Header: CoAP uses a compact binary header, reducing the protocol overhead.

f. Multicast Support: CoAP allows for efficient group communication through multicast messages.

3. Use Cases for CoAP:

- **Smart Grids:** CoAP is used in smart grid applications to enable communication between smart meters, grid equipment, and utility servers.

- **Wearable Devices:** CoAP is suitable for wearable IoT devices that need to transmit data efficiently over constrained networks.

- **Industrial Automation:** CoAP is employed in industrial automation scenarios, facilitating communication between sensors, actuators, and controllers.

Conclusion:

MQTT and CoAP are two essential communication protocols that underpin the IoT ecosystem. By offering efficient, lightweight, and reliable communication, they enable a wide range of IoT applications, from smart homes to industrial automation. The choice between MQTT and CoAP often depends on the specific requirements and constraints of the IoT project, emphasizing the importance of understanding their capabilities and use cases in building robust and efficient IoT solutions.

B. HTTP and REST for IoT: Leveraging Web Principles for Seamless Connectivity

HTTP (Hypertext Transfer Protocol) and REST (Representational State Transfer) are fundamental technologies that have found a significant place in the Internet of Things (IoT) landscape. Leveraging these web-based principles, HTTP and REST enable the interaction and communication of IoT devices and systems in a standardized, efficient, and scalable manner. In this exploration, we delve into the intricacies of HTTP and REST in the context of IoT, unraveling their significance, key features, use cases, and how they contribute to the seamless connectivity that powers the IoT ecosystem.

HTTP (Hypertext Transfer Protocol):

1. Significance of HTTP in IoT:

HTTP, the foundation of the World Wide Web, is a well-established protocol for data transfer between clients (such as web browsers) and servers. Its widespread adoption and compatibility make it a valuable tool for enabling IoT devices to interact with web services, cloud platforms, and applications.

2. Key Features of HTTP in IoT:

a. Request-Response Model: HTTP operates on a request-response model, where IoT devices can send requests to servers (GET, POST, PUT, DELETE) and receive responses.

b. Standardization: HTTP is a standardized protocol with well-defined methods, status codes, and headers, ensuring consistency in communication.

c. Familiarity: Developers are already familiar with HTTP due to its extensive use on the web, making it accessible for IoT application development.

d. Scalability: HTTP is inherently scalable, allowing IoT devices to communicate with numerous servers and services simultaneously.

e. Security: HTTPS (HTTP Secure) adds a layer of security through encryption, ensuring the confidentiality and integrity of data exchanged.

3. Use Cases for HTTP in IoT:

- **IoT Device Management:** HTTP is used to manage and configure IoT devices remotely.

- **Data Upload to the Cloud:** IoT devices can use HTTP to upload sensor data to cloud platforms for storage and analysis.

- **Web-Based Dashboards:** HTTP facilitates the creation of web-based dashboards that visualize and control IoT devices.

REST (Representational State Transfer):

1. Significance of REST in IoT:

REST is an architectural style for designing networked applications that leverage the principles of the web. In IoT, RESTful APIs provide a uniform and scalable approach for accessing and manipulating resources, making it easier for developers to build interoperable and web-like IoT systems.

2. Key Features of REST in IoT:

a. Resource-Centric: REST treats everything as a resource, such as IoT devices, sensors, and data points, which can be identified by unique URLs.

b. Stateless: Each request from a client to a server in REST must contain all the information needed to understand and process it. This statelessness simplifies communication.

c. CRUD Operations: RESTful APIs support the standard Create, Read, Update, and Delete (CRUD) operations, making it intuitive for developers to work with resources.

d. Self-Descriptive Messages: RESTful responses contain information that describes how to process them, enabling discoverability and ease of use.

e. Interoperability: REST's simplicity and adherence to web principles promote interoperability and compatibility among IoT devices and services.

3. Use Cases for REST in IoT:

- **IoT Device Control:** RESTful APIs allow IoT devices to be controlled and monitored through web-based interfaces.

- **Resource Discovery:** IoT devices can expose their capabilities and data via REST APIs, enabling dynamic resource discovery.

- **Data Retrieval:** IoT devices can provide historical data and real-time sensor readings through REST endpoints.

Conclusion:

HTTP and REST are foundational technologies that bring the principles of the web to the IoT realm, enabling standardized, efficient, and scalable communication. By leveraging these technologies, IoT devices can interact seamlessly with web services, cloud platforms, and applications, opening up a world of possibilities for building interconnected and interoperable IoT ecosystems. Understanding their capabilities and use cases is crucial for developers and organizations aiming to harness the full potential of IoT in our digitally connected world.

C. DDS (Data Distribution Service): Enabling Real-Time Data Exchange in Complex Systems

DDS, or Data Distribution Service, is an advanced and standardized messaging protocol designed for real-time, high-performance data distribution in complex and distributed systems, making it a crucial technology in the Internet of Things (IoT) landscape. DDS ensures reliable, efficient, and scalable communication between devices, sensors, and applications, even in challenging and dynamic environments. In this exploration, we delve into the intricacies of DDS, unraveling its significance, key features, use cases, and how it contributes to the seamless and responsive data exchange that powers mission-critical IoT applications.

1. Significance of DDS in IoT:

DDS plays a pivotal role in IoT by addressing the need for timely and reliable data exchange between a multitude of devices, often distributed across vast networks. It is particularly valuable in scenarios where low-latency, high-throughput, and guaranteed delivery of data are critical, such as industrial automation, smart grids, and autonomous vehicles.

2. Key Features of DDS:

a. Publish-Subscribe Model: DDS employs a publish-subscribe communication pattern, allowing data producers (publishers) to send information to specific data consumers (subscribers) based on their interests. This decoupling of producers and consumers enhances flexibility and scalability.

b. Real-Time Data: DDS is optimized for real-time data exchange, ensuring that data is delivered with minimal latency, making it suitable for applications that require immediate responses.

c. Quality of Service (QoS): DDS provides a robust QoS mechanism that allows users to define parameters for data reliability, delivery deadlines, and resource management. This ensures that data delivery meets application requirements.

d. Data-Centric Design: DDS focuses on data rather than the transport or network layer, allowing applications to express their data needs and priorities directly.

e. Dynamic Discovery: DDS supports dynamic discovery of data sources and consumers, making it suitable for dynamic and changing environments where devices come and go.

f. Extensibility: DDS is designed to be extensible, allowing developers to define custom data types and behaviors to suit specific application needs.

3. Use Cases for DDS in IoT:

- **Industrial IoT (IIoT):** DDS is extensively used in industrial automation and control systems to ensure real-time communication between sensors, actuators, and controllers.

- **Autonomous Vehicles:** DDS enables real-time data exchange among sensors (e.g., lidar, radar), control systems, and decision-making modules in autonomous vehicles.

- **Healthcare:** In telemedicine and remote patient monitoring, DDS ensures the timely and reliable transmission of patient data.

- **Aerospace and Defense:** DDS is used in military and aerospace applications for real-time data sharing between mission-critical systems.

4. DDS Implementations:

- **OpenDDS:** An open-source DDS implementation developed by Object Computing, Inc.

- **RTI Connext:** A commercial DDS solution provided by Real-Time Innovations (RTI), known for its performance and reliability.

- **eProsima Fast DDS:** An open-source DDS implementation that aims to provide a lightweight and efficient solution.

5. Future Trends:

- Integration with edge computing to support IoT applications requiring low latency and data processing at the edge.

- Adoption of DDS in 5G networks to enable real-time data exchange in the emerging era of ultra-reliable low-latency communication (URLLC).

Conclusion:

DDS is a powerful and standardized protocol that excels in facilitating real-time data exchange in complex and distributed systems, making it a cornerstone technology in the IoT landscape. By providing low-latency, high-throughput, and configurable data delivery, DDS ensures that IoT applications can respond to dynamic and mission-critical requirements, spanning industries from industrial automation to healthcare and beyond. Understanding its capabilities and use cases is essential for developers and organizations aiming to harness the full potential of real-time data exchange in IoT applications.

D. IoT Protocol Selection Criteria: Choosing the Right Communication Framework for Connected Devices

Selecting the appropriate communication protocol is a pivotal decision in the development of IoT (Internet of Things) solutions. IoT protocols define how devices communicate, exchange data, and interact within an ecosystem. The choice of protocol significantly impacts factors like device performance, scalability, security, and interoperability. To make an informed decision, developers and IoT stakeholders must consider a set of key criteria when evaluating and selecting an IoT communication protocol.

1. Data Characteristics:

- **Data Volume:** Consider the amount of data your IoT devices will generate and transmit. Low-power devices with limited bandwidth may require protocols optimized for minimal data transmission, while high-data devices may demand higher throughput protocols.

- **Data Rate:** Determine whether your application requires real-time or periodic data updates. Some protocols are optimized for low latency and real-time data, while others are more suited for periodic or batch updates.

- **Data Type:** Consider the type of data being transmitted. Is it telemetry data, sensor readings, multimedia content, or control commands? Some protocols are better suited for specific data types.

2. Device Characteristics:

- **Resource Constraints:** Evaluate the processing power, memory, and energy constraints of your IoT devices. Low-power, resource-constrained devices may require lightweight protocols designed for efficiency.

- **Device Heterogeneity:** Consider the diversity of devices in your IoT ecosystem. Some protocols are better at accommodating heterogeneous device types and capabilities.

3. Reliability and Quality of Service (QoS):

- **Reliability:** Assess the reliability requirements of your application. Some IoT applications, like industrial control systems, require guaranteed message delivery, while others, like environmental monitoring, may tolerate occasional data loss.

- **Quality of Service (QoS):** Determine the required QoS levels, including delivery guarantees, message prioritization, and resource management. Some protocols offer configurable QoS to align with application needs.

4. Security:

- **Authentication:** Evaluate the protocol's support for device authentication and identity verification to prevent unauthorized access.

- **Encryption:** Ensure data privacy by selecting protocols that support data encryption for secure transmission.

- **Access Control:** Consider access control mechanisms for securing data and resources within your IoT ecosystem.

5. Scalability:

- **Network Size:** Determine the scale of your IoT deployment. Some protocols are better suited for small-scale deployments, while others are designed to handle large-scale, global IoT networks.

- **Topology:** Consider the network topology (star, mesh, peer-to-peer) of your IoT ecosystem. Protocols should support the intended network architecture.

6. Interoperability:

- **Standards Compliance:** Favor protocols that adhere to established industry standards and specifications, promoting interoperability between devices and platforms.

- **Open Source:** Open-source protocols may offer greater flexibility and adaptability, especially in multi-vendor IoT environments.

7. Latency and Timing:

- **Latency Tolerance:** Assess your application's tolerance for message delivery latency. Some IoT protocols prioritize low-latency communication.

- **Timing Requirements:** Determine whether your IoT system requires synchronous or asynchronous communication.

8. Power Efficiency:

- **Battery Life:** For battery-powered devices, consider the protocol's impact on power consumption. Protocols designed for low-power devices can extend battery life.

9. Ecosystem Support:

- **Developer Community:** Evaluate the size and activity of the protocol's developer community. A thriving community can provide valuable resources, libraries, and support.

- **Platform Integration:** Ensure that the protocol is supported by the platforms, cloud services, and middleware you plan to use.

10. Cost and Licensing:

- **Licensing Fees:** Consider any licensing fees associated with proprietary protocols, as they can impact the overall cost of your IoT solution.

11. Future Proofing:

- **Evolution:** Assess the protocol's roadmap and its ability to accommodate future IoT advancements, such as 5G, edge computing, and emerging technologies.

In conclusion, the selection of an IoT communication protocol is a critical decision that should align with the specific requirements, constraints, and objectives of your IoT application. A thorough evaluation of these criteria will help you choose the right protocol, ensuring the success and effectiveness of your IoT solution.

E. IoT Interoperability: Bridging the Connectivity Divide in the Internet of Things

Interoperability is a cornerstone of the Internet of Things (IoT) that ensures different devices, systems, and applications can seamlessly communicate and work together within the IoT ecosystem. In a world where billions of diverse IoT devices are connected, interoperability is paramount for maximizing the potential of IoT, enabling data sharing, and fostering innovation. In this exploration, we delve into the intricacies of IoT interoperability, its significance, challenges, key approaches, and how it bridges the connectivity divide in the ever-expanding IoT landscape.

1. Significance of IoT Interoperability:

- **Holistic Connectivity:** IoT devices come from various manufacturers and employ different communication protocols and data formats. Interoperability ensures these devices can communicate and collaborate, forming a holistic IoT network.

- **Scalability:** Interoperability allows IoT ecosystems to scale efficiently by integrating new devices and technologies without significant disruptions.

- **Data Insights:** Data from diverse IoT sources can be combined and analyzed to extract valuable insights, driving informed decision-making.

- **Innovation:** Interoperability fosters innovation by encouraging the development of new applications and services that leverage the combined capabilities of diverse IoT devices.

2. Key Challenges in IoT Interoperability:

- **Diverse Standards:** The IoT landscape is characterized by a multitude of communication protocols, data formats, and standards. Achieving interoperability between these diverse technologies can be complex.

- **Security Concerns:** Ensuring security when connecting heterogeneous devices is challenging, as vulnerabilities in one device can potentially compromise the entire ecosystem.

- **Legacy Systems:** Many existing IoT devices may not support modern interoperability standards, making integration with legacy systems a challenge.

- **Scalability:** As IoT ecosystems grow, maintaining interoperability at scale becomes increasingly difficult.

3. Approaches to IoT Interoperability:

- **Standardization:** Developing and adhering to common standards for communication protocols, data formats, and security mechanisms is a fundamental approach to achieving interoperability. Prominent standards organizations like the IoT Consortium (IoTC), IEEE, and IETF play a crucial role in this regard.

- **Middleware and APIs:** Middleware solutions and well-defined application programming interfaces (APIs) can bridge the gap between different devices and platforms, allowing them to communicate with one another.

- **Gateways:** Gateways serve as intermediaries between devices that use different protocols, translating data and enabling communication.

- **Semantic Interoperability:** Ensuring that data shared between devices has common meaning and context, often facilitated by using semantic technologies like RDF (Resource Description Framework) and ontologies.

- **Edge Computing:** Edge computing can enhance interoperability by processing and filtering data at the edge of the network, reducing the burden on centralized systems.

4. Industry Initiatives:

- **OneM2M:** A global standards initiative for M2M (Machine-to-Machine) and IoT interoperability, aiming to provide a common platform for IoT applications.

- **Open Connectivity Foundation (OCF):** Focused on creating a common IoT standard for secure device interoperability and data exchange.

- **Thread Group:** An industry alliance that develops networking technologies for IoT, with an emphasis on interoperability and security.

5. Future Trends in IoT Interoperability:

- **AI and Machine Learning:** Integration of AI-driven solutions to enhance IoT interoperability, automate device discovery, and optimize data integration.

- **Blockchain:** Leveraging blockchain technology for secure and transparent data sharing and device interactions in IoT.

- **5G Networks:** The rollout of 5G networks is expected to provide the high bandwidth and low latency required for seamless IoT interoperability.

- **Edge Computing:** Increased adoption of edge computing to process data locally and reduce latency, enhancing real-time interoperability.

Conclusion:

IoT interoperability is the linchpin that enables the diverse and expansive IoT ecosystem to function harmoniously. By addressing the challenges through standardization, middleware, and emerging technologies, the IoT industry is poised to achieve greater levels of interoperability, unlocking new opportunities for innovation, data-driven insights, and the realization of the full potential of the Internet of Things.

CHAPTER 9

IoT Use Cases and Applications

The Internet of Things (IoT) has ushered in a new era of innovation, transforming industries, cities, and our daily lives. At the heart of this transformation are the countless use cases and applications that leverage the connectivity and intelligence of IoT devices. From smart cities to industrial automation, healthcare to agriculture, IoT has woven its presence into nearly every facet of our world. In this exploration, we embark on a journey through the vast landscape of IoT use cases and applications, uncovering the real-world scenarios where IoT is making a profound impact and reshaping our future. Welcome to the realm of IoT possibilities, where connected devices are revolutionizing the way we live, work, and interact with the world around us.

A. Smart Cities: Transforming Urban Living Through IoT

Smart cities represent a visionary and transformative concept, harnessing the power of the Internet of Things (IoT) to revolutionize urban living, enhance sustainability, and improve the quality of life for citizens. These connected metropolises leverage IoT technologies to collect, analyze, and act upon data from various sources, from sensors on streetlights to citizens' smartphones, in order to optimize infrastructure, services, and resource management. In this exploration, we delve into the intricacies of smart cities, their significance, key components, challenges, and the ways in which they are reshaping the urban landscape.

1. Significance of Smart Cities:

- **Efficiency and Sustainability:** Smart cities aim to optimize resource utilization, reduce energy consumption, and minimize environmental impact, promoting sustainability and resilience in the face of urban growth.

- **Improved Quality of Life:** By enhancing public services, transportation, healthcare, and safety, smart cities aspire to improve the overall well-being and quality of life for their residents.

- **Economic Growth:** Smart city initiatives can stimulate economic development by attracting businesses, startups, and innovation hubs that leverage IoT technologies.

2. Key Components of Smart Cities:

- **IoT Sensors:** Smart cities deploy a multitude of sensors to collect real-time data on air quality, traffic flow, waste management, energy consumption, and more.

- **Data Analytics:** Advanced data analytics and artificial intelligence (AI) processes the collected data to gain insights, predict trends, and optimize resource allocation.

- **Connectivity:** Robust and high-speed connectivity, such as 5G networks, is essential for enabling real-time data transmission and communication between devices.

- **Integrated Systems:** Smart cities integrate disparate systems, such as transportation, energy, healthcare, and public safety, to enable efficient coordination and decision-making.

- **Citizen Engagement:** Engaging citizens through digital platforms and mobile apps fosters a sense of participation and allows them to provide feedback and access city services.

3. IoT Applications in Smart Cities:

- **Smart Transportation:** IoT-enabled traffic management, connected vehicles, and intelligent public transportation systems reduce congestion and enhance mobility.

- **Sustainable Energy:** Smart grids and energy management systems optimize energy consumption, reduce waste, and integrate renewable energy sources.

- **Environmental Monitoring:** IoT sensors track air and water quality, detect pollution, and provide early warnings for natural disasters.

- **Waste Management:** Smart waste bins equipped with sensors optimize garbage collection routes, reducing costs and environmental impact.

- **Public Safety:** IoT surveillance cameras, gunshot detectors, and emergency response systems enhance public safety and disaster preparedness.

- **Healthcare:** Remote patient monitoring, wearable health devices, and telemedicine services improve healthcare accessibility and outcomes.

4. Challenges in Smart City Implementation:

- **Data Privacy and Security:** Handling sensitive citizen data requires robust security measures and privacy protection.

- **Infrastructure Investment:** Building the necessary IoT infrastructure and networks can be capital-intensive.

- **Interoperability:** Ensuring that diverse IoT systems and devices can communicate and work together is a challenge.

- **Citizen Engagement:** Encouraging citizen participation and overcoming potential resistance to change are ongoing challenges.

5. Future Trends in Smart Cities:

- **Edge Computing:** Edge computing will enable real-time data processing at the edge of the network, reducing latency and enhancing responsiveness.

- **AI and Machine Learning:** The use of AI algorithms will become more sophisticated in predicting and managing urban processes.

- **Blockchain:** Blockchain technology may play a role in securing data and transactions in smart cities.

- **Digital Twins:** Digital twin technology will create virtual replicas of cities to simulate and optimize various scenarios.

Conclusion:

Smart cities represent a paradigm shift in urban planning and governance, driven by IoT technologies. By harnessing data-driven insights, connectivity, and citizen engagement, these cities aspire to create more sustainable, efficient, and livable environments. While challenges exist, the vision of smart cities continues to inspire innovation and shape the urban landscape of the future, where technology is seamlessly integrated into our daily lives for the betterment of all.

B. Industrial IoT (IIoT): Transforming Industries Through Connectivity and Data

Industrial Internet of Things (IIoT) is a transformative

technology that leverages the power of connectivity, data, and automation to revolutionize industrial processes and operations. IIoT extends the capabilities of traditional industries by connecting devices, machines, and systems to the internet, enabling real-time monitoring, data analysis, and informed decision-making. In this exploration, we delve into the intricacies of IIoT, its significance, key components, applications, challenges, and how it is reshaping industries across the globe.

1. Significance of Industrial IoT (IIoT):

- **Efficiency and Productivity:** IIoT optimizes industrial processes, streamlines operations, reduces downtime, and enhances productivity.

- **Cost Reduction:** IIoT can lead to significant cost savings through predictive maintenance, resource optimization, and energy efficiency.

- **Quality and Safety:** Real-time monitoring and control improve product quality and ensure safer working environments.

- **Competitive Advantage:** IIoT enables data-driven insights, providing a competitive edge by identifying opportunities for innovation and process improvement.

2. Key Components of IIoT:

- **Sensors and Actuators:** These devices collect data from the physical environment and can trigger actions based on received information.

- **Connectivity:** Robust and secure connectivity, such as wired (Ethernet) or wireless (Wi-Fi, cellular, LoRa), enables data transmission from devices to centralized systems.

- **Data Analytics:** Advanced analytics platforms process and analyze data to extract actionable insights and make informed decisions.

- **Cloud Computing:** Cloud services store and manage large volumes of IIoT data, provide computing resources, and offer scalable solutions.

- **Edge Computing:** Edge devices process data locally, reducing latency and ensuring real-time responses in critical applications.

3. IIoT Applications:

- **Predictive Maintenance:** IIoT sensors monitor equipment conditions, enabling predictive maintenance to prevent breakdowns and reduce downtime.

- **Supply Chain Optimization:** Real-time tracking of goods and assets across the supply chain enhances visibility, reduces delays, and improves inventory management.

- **Energy Management:** IIoT systems optimize energy consumption by monitoring and controlling devices and systems.

- **Quality Control:** Continuous monitoring and data analysis during manufacturing processes improve product quality and reduce defects.

- **Remote Monitoring and Control:** IIoT enables remote monitoring and control of industrial processes, enhancing safety and efficiency.

4. Challenges in IIoT Implementation:

- **Security:** Protecting sensitive industrial data and ensuring the security of connected devices is a top concern.

- **Legacy Systems:** Integrating IIoT into existing industrial systems and equipment can be challenging.

- **Interoperability:** Ensuring compatibility between diverse IIoT devices and systems is crucial.

- **Scalability:** As IIoT deployments grow, managing and scaling the infrastructure can become complex.

5. Future Trends in IIoT:

- **5G Connectivity:** High-speed, low-latency 5G networks will facilitate real-time data transmission and support mission-critical IIoT applications.

- **AI and Machine Learning:** AI algorithms will become increasingly sophisticated in analyzing and predicting industrial processes.

- **Digital Twins:** Digital twin technology will create virtual replicas of industrial systems for simulation, optimization, and predictive maintenance.

- **Blockchain:** Blockchain may find applications in IIoT for secure data sharing, supply chain tracking, and more.

Conclusion:

IIoT is driving a significant shift in industrial processes, ushering in a new era of data-driven decision-making, efficiency, and innovation. By connecting industrial devices, harnessing data analytics, and leveraging emerging technologies, IIoT is poised to reshape industries, foster sustainability, and redefine the way businesses operate in the 21st century. As challenges are addressed and technology advances, the full potential of IIoT is expected to continue unfolding, enabling smarter, more efficient, and more competitive industrial operations.

C. Healthcare and Wearables: Empowering Wellness through IoT Technology

The convergence of healthcare and wearable technology within the Internet of Things (IoT) has revolutionized the way individuals monitor and manage their health. Wearable devices equipped with sensors, connectivity, and data analytics have enabled real-time health tracking, early disease detection, and improved patient care. In this exploration, we delve into the intricacies of healthcare and wearables, their significance, key components, applications, challenges, and the transformative impact they have on healthcare delivery and personal well-being.

1. Significance of Healthcare and Wearables:

- **Preventive Healthcare:** Wearables promote a proactive approach to health by providing users with continuous, real-time data about their vital signs, physical activity, and overall well-being.

- **Chronic Disease Management:** Patients with chronic conditions, such as diabetes or hypertension, can monitor their health remotely, reducing the need for frequent clinic visits.

- **Healthcare Accessibility:** Wearable devices extend healthcare services to underserved populations and remote areas, enhancing access to medical expertise.

- **Data-Driven Medicine:** Wearable-generated data contributes to personalized healthcare, allowing clinicians to tailor treatments and interventions based on individual health metrics.

2. Key Components of Healthcare Wearables:

- **Sensors:** These devices incorporate various sensors, such as heart rate monitors, accelerometers, ECG sensors, and temperature sensors, to collect health-related data.

- **Connectivity:** Wearables use Bluetooth, Wi-Fi, or cellular connectivity to transmit data to smartphones, tablets, or cloud-based platforms for analysis.

- **Battery:** Long battery life is essential for continuous monitoring and user convenience.

- **Data Analytics:** Advanced data analytics software processes and interprets the data, providing users and healthcare professionals with actionable insights.

- **User Interface:** An intuitive user interface, often through a smartphone app, allows users to visualize and understand their health data.

3. Healthcare and Wearables Applications:

- **Fitness Tracking:** Wearables monitor physical activity, calories burned, sleep quality, and provide insights to help users achieve fitness goals.

- **Remote Patient Monitoring:** Patients with chronic diseases can track their vital signs, and healthcare providers can remotely monitor patient health.

- **Medication Adherence:** Wearables can send medication reminders and track adherence, improving medication management for patients.

- **Emergency Alerts:** Fall detection and vital sign monitoring can trigger emergency alerts to caregivers or medical professionals.

- **Disease Detection:** Wearables can detect early signs of diseases like atrial fibrillation, sleep apnea, or diabetes.

4. Challenges in Healthcare Wearables:

- **Data Privacy and Security:** Protecting sensitive health data is paramount, requiring robust security measures and compliance with healthcare regulations.

- **Data Accuracy:** Ensuring the accuracy of wearable-generated data is crucial for reliable health monitoring and diagnosis.

- **User Adoption:** Encouraging users to consistently wear and engage with these devices can be a challenge.

- **Regulatory Compliance:** Healthcare wearables must adhere to strict regulatory guidelines to ensure safety and efficacy.

5. Future Trends in Healthcare Wearables:

- **Advanced Sensors:** Integration of more advanced sensors for monitoring additional health parameters.

- **AI and Machine Learning:** Enhanced AI algorithms for more accurate data interpretation and predictive health insights.

- **Integration with Telemedicine:** Seamless integration of wearables with telemedicine platforms for remote consultations.

- **Medical-Grade Devices:** The development of medical-grade wearables for clinical-grade monitoring and diagnosis.

Conclusion:

Healthcare wearables are ushering in a new era of personalized health management and preventive medicine. By providing individuals with real-time health data and connecting them with healthcare professionals, these devices empower users to take control of their well-being. Challenges remain in terms of data privacy and accuracy, but as technology evolves, healthcare wearables are poised to become indispensable tools for both consumers and the medical community, ultimately improving healthcare outcomes and quality of life.

D. Agriculture and Environmental Monitoring: Cultivating Sustainability with IoT

Agriculture and environmental monitoring are two critical domains that have embraced the Internet of Things (IoT) to enhance resource management, improve crop yields, and mitigate environmental challenges. IoT technology, through the deployment of sensors, data analytics, and real-time monitoring, has transformed traditional farming practices and enabled precision agriculture. In this exploration, we delve into the intricacies of agriculture and environmental monitoring, their significance, key components, applications, challenges, and the profound impact they have on sustainable agriculture and ecological preservation.

1. Significance of Agriculture and Environmental Monitoring:

- **Precision Agriculture:** IoT technology empowers farmers to make data-driven decisions, optimizing resource allocation, and increasing crop yield while reducing waste.

- **Resource Conservation:** Monitoring environmental conditions helps conserve valuable resources such as water and energy, critical in the face of climate change and resource scarcity.

- **Environmental Preservation:** IoT contributes to the preservation of ecosystems and biodiversity by monitoring and mitigating the impact of human activities on the environment.

- **Food Security:** Improved agriculture practices enabled by IoT can help ensure global food security by increasing production efficiency.

2. Key Components of Agriculture and Environmental Monitoring:

- **Sensors:** These devices include soil moisture sensors, weather stations, drones, and satellite imagery that collect data on environmental conditions.

- **Connectivity:** IoT networks and protocols enable real-time data transmission from sensors to centralized systems for analysis.

- **Data Analytics:** Advanced data analytics software processes and interprets data to provide actionable insights for farmers and environmental scientists.

- **Automation:** IoT technology can automate tasks such as irrigation, pest control, and harvesting based on data-driven insights.

3. Agriculture and Environmental Monitoring Applications:

- **Precision Agriculture:** IoT-enabled devices monitor soil conditions, crop health, and weather patterns, enabling precise application of water, fertilizers, and pesticides.

- **Weather Forecasting:** IoT weather stations provide real-time weather data, aiding in weather forecasting and disaster preparedness.

- **Water Management:** Sensors monitor water quality and usage in irrigation systems, ensuring efficient water utilization and reducing water waste.

- **Biodiversity Conservation:** IoT assists in tracking and monitoring endangered species and ecosystems, contributing to biodiversity preservation.

- **Environmental Pollution Monitoring:** Sensors detect pollutants in air and water, helping to monitor and combat environmental pollution.

4. Challenges in Agriculture and Environmental Monitoring:

- **Data Management:** Handling vast amounts of data generated by sensors requires robust data management and storage solutions.

- **Data Privacy and Security:** Protecting sensitive environmental and agricultural data is crucial, necessitating stringent security measures.

- **Cost of Implementation:** Initial setup costs and maintenance of IoT systems can be a barrier, particularly for small-scale farmers.

- **Interoperability:** Ensuring compatibility between diverse IoT devices and systems is essential for seamless monitoring.

5. Future Trends in Agriculture and Environmental Monitoring:

- **Satellite IoT:** Integration of satellite technology into IoT networks for wider coverage and remote monitoring of remote and rural areas.

- **AI and Machine Learning:** Enhanced AI algorithms for more accurate data interpretation, predictive analysis, and automated decision-making.

- **Blockchain:** Employing blockchain for transparent and tamper-proof record-keeping in environmental monitoring and supply chain management.

- **Urban Agriculture:** IoT will play a significant role in urban farming and vertical agriculture, addressing food security challenges in densely populated areas.

Conclusion:

Agriculture and environmental monitoring through IoT are ushering in an era of sustainable farming practices and ecological preservation. By providing real-time data and insights, IoT empowers farmers, environmentalists, and policymakers to make informed decisions and take proactive measures. Challenges persist in terms of data management and security, but as technology continues to advance, agriculture and environmental monitoring will play an indispensable role in achieving a more sustainable and resilient future for both agriculture and the environment.

E. Consumer IoT: Transforming Daily Life with Smart Homes and IoT Wearables

Consumer Internet of Things (IoT) represents a revolution in how people interact with technology in their daily lives. Smart homes and IoT wearables are two primary segments of consumer IoT that have gained widespread adoption. These technologies leverage connectivity, data analytics, and automation to enhance convenience, comfort, and overall well-being. In this exploration, we delve into the intricacies of consumer IoT, its significance, key components, applications, challenges, and the transformative impact it has on the way people live, work, and play.

1. Significance of Consumer IoT:

- **Convenience:** Consumer IoT devices simplify daily tasks and routines, providing convenience and automation in homes and on-the-go.

- **Personalization:** IoT wearables and smart home devices offer personalized experiences tailored to individual preferences and needs.

- **Energy Efficiency:** Smart homes help reduce energy consumption and lower utility bills through intelligent management of lighting, heating, and cooling.

- **Health and Wellness:** IoT wearables promote health and fitness by tracking vital signs, physical activity, and providing valuable health insights.

2. Key Components of Consumer IoT:

- **Sensors:** Smart home devices and wearables are equipped with various sensors, such as motion sensors, temperature sensors, heart rate monitors, and GPS.

- **Connectivity:** IoT devices use Wi-Fi, Bluetooth, Zigbee, or cellular connectivity to communicate with other devices and central control hubs.

- **Data Analytics:** Advanced data analytics processes data generated by IoT devices, providing insights and enabling automation.

- **User Interface:** Smartphone apps, voice assistants, and user interfaces on IoT devices allow users to interact and control devices.

- **Automation:** IoT devices can automate tasks, such as adjusting thermostats, turning on lights, or sending notifications based on user-defined rules.

3. Consumer IoT Applications:

Smart Homes:

- **Home Automation:** Smart homes automate lighting, heating, cooling, and security systems, enhancing energy efficiency and security.

- **Voice Assistants:** Devices like Amazon Echo and Google Home enable voice control of smart home devices and provide information and entertainment.

- **Security and Surveillance:** Smart cameras, doorbells, and sensors enhance home security, allowing remote monitoring and alerts.

- **Entertainment:** IoT devices offer seamless streaming, gaming, and audio experiences through connected entertainment systems.

IoT Wearables:

- **Health and Fitness:** Smartwatches and fitness trackers monitor heart rate, sleep, physical activity, and provide health insights.

- **Notifications:** Wearables deliver notifications, messages, and alerts, reducing the need to check smartphones frequently.

- **Navigation:** Smart glasses and augmented reality headsets provide navigation and contextual information.

- **Personal Safety:** Wearables offer safety features, such as fall detection, SOS alerts, and location tracking.

4. Challenges in Consumer IoT:

- **Interoperability:** Ensuring compatibility between devices from different manufacturers can be challenging.

- **Data Privacy and Security:** Protecting user data and ensuring device security is crucial, given the sensitive nature of IoT data.

- **User Adoption:** Encouraging users to embrace and trust IoT technology can be a hurdle.

- **Device Lifecycle:** IoT devices may become obsolete quickly, leading to electronic waste and sustainability concerns.

5. Future Trends in Consumer IoT:

- **5G Connectivity:** High-speed, low-latency 5G networks will enhance IoT device performance and capabilities.

- **AI and Machine Learning:** AI algorithms will provide more personalized and intelligent interactions with IoT devices.

- **Healthcare Integration:** IoT wearables will play a more significant role in remote healthcare monitoring and diagnosis.

- **Smart Cities Integration:** Consumer IoT will become more integrated with smart city ecosystems, enhancing urban living.

Conclusion:

Consumer IoT is reshaping daily life by bringing technology into the home and on the body. Smart homes and IoT wearables offer convenience, personalization, and improved well-being. Challenges related to security, interoperability, and user adoption persist, but as technology continues to evolve, consumer IoT will play an increasingly central role in how people live, work, and experience the world around them.

F. Automotive and Transportation: Pioneering Mobility Through IoT Innovation

The fusion of the Internet of Things (IoT) with the automotive and transportation industries has ushered in a transformative era of connected vehicles, intelligent transportation systems, and enhanced safety and efficiency. IoT technology has redefined the way we move, travel, and manage transportation networks. In this exploration, we delve into the intricacies of automotive and transportation IoT, its significance, key components, applications, challenges, and the profound impact it has on modern mobility and transportation systems.

1. Significance of Automotive and Transportation IoT:

- **Enhanced Safety:** IoT-enabled vehicles and transportation systems provide real-time data and connectivity, contributing to safer roads and reduced accidents.

- **Efficiency:** Connected vehicles optimize fuel consumption, reduce traffic congestion, and improve transportation logistics, leading to resource and time savings.

- **Sustainability:** IoT supports eco-friendly transportation solutions, such as electric vehicles and reduced emissions through optimized traffic flow.

- **Customer Experience:** IoT technology offers enhanced in-vehicle infotainment, navigation, and personalized services, improving the passenger experience.

2. Key Components of Automotive and Transportation IoT:

- **Connected Vehicles:** These are equipped with sensors, GPS, and communication modules that enable data collection and communication with other vehicles and infrastructure.

- **IoT Networks:** High-speed cellular networks and emerging 5G technology provide the connectivity backbone for connected vehicles.

- **Data Analytics:** Advanced data analytics processes vehicle data for predictive maintenance, traffic management, and safety.

- **Intelligent Transportation Systems (ITS):** Infrastructure components like smart traffic lights, road sensors, and vehicle-to-infrastructure (V2I) communication enable real-time traffic management.

- **Cybersecurity:** IoT security measures are essential to protect connected vehicles from cyber threats and ensure data privacy.

3. Automotive and Transportation IoT Applications:

- **Connected Vehicles:** IoT-enabled vehicles communicate with each other (vehicle-to-vehicle or V2V) and with infrastructure

(V2I) to improve traffic flow, reduce accidents, and optimize routes.

- **Fleet Management:** IoT technology tracks and manages commercial vehicle fleets, improving efficiency, fuel economy, and maintenance.

- **Smart Traffic Management:** IoT-based traffic lights and road sensors optimize traffic flow, reduce congestion, and improve road safety.

- **Navigation and Mapping:** IoT-powered GPS and navigation systems offer real-time traffic updates, route optimization, and accurate mapping.

- **Vehicle Diagnostics:** IoT sensors monitor vehicle performance, detect issues, and schedule maintenance, reducing breakdowns and repair costs.

4. Challenges in Automotive and Transportation IoT:

- **Security Concerns:** Protecting connected vehicles from cyberattacks and ensuring data privacy is a top priority.

- **Standardization:** Establishing common standards and protocols for IoT devices and systems is essential for interoperability.

- **Data Overload:** Handling the massive volumes of data

generated by IoT devices requires robust data management and analytics.

- **Infrastructure Development:** Building the necessary infrastructure, including IoT networks and V2I communication, can be costly and time-consuming.

5. Future Trends in Automotive and Transportation IoT:

- **Autonomous Vehicles:** IoT will play a pivotal role in the development and deployment of autonomous vehicles, enabling real-time communication and coordination.

- **Smart Cities Integration:** IoT-connected transportation systems will become more integrated with smart city initiatives, reducing traffic congestion and emissions.

- **Mobility as a Service (MaaS):** IoT will support the rise of MaaS platforms, providing seamless, on-demand transportation options.

- **Environmental Sustainability:** IoT will continue to drive eco-friendly transportation solutions, including electric vehicles and shared mobility.

Conclusion:

Automotive and transportation IoT is revolutionizing how we move people and goods. Connected vehicles and intelligent transportation systems are enhancing safety, efficiency, and sustainability while offering passengers improved experiences. Challenges remain, particularly in cybersecurity and standardization, but as technology continues to advance, automotive and transportation IoT will play an increasingly vital role in shaping the future of mobility and transportation systems.

G. Energy and Utilities: Powering Sustainability and Efficiency Through IoT

The convergence of the Internet of Things (IoT) with the energy and utilities sector has brought about a paradigm shift in how we generate, distribute, and consume energy. IoT technology has transformed power grids into smart grids, enabling greater efficiency, sustainability, and reliability. In this exploration, we delve into the intricacies of energy and utilities IoT, its significance, key components, applications, challenges, and the profound impact it has on modern energy management and utility services.

1. Significance of Energy and Utilities IoT:

- **Efficiency:** IoT-enabled smart grids and utility management systems optimize energy distribution, reduce wastage, and enhance resource utilization.

- **Sustainability:** Renewable energy integration and real-time monitoring of energy consumption contribute to reduced greenhouse gas emissions and a more sustainable future.

- **Reliability:** IoT technology improves grid resilience, reduces downtime, and enhances power quality, leading to more reliable utility services.

- **Cost Savings:** Smart meters and demand response systems enable cost-effective utility management and reduced energy bills for consumers.

2. Key Components of Energy and Utilities IoT:

- **Smart Meters:** These devices collect real-time data on energy consumption and enable two-way communication between consumers and utilities.

- **IoT Sensors:** Sensors placed on power lines, transformers, and substations monitor voltage, current, temperature, and humidity, providing valuable data for grid management.

- **Communication Networks:** Robust and secure communication networks enable data transmission between devices and centralized utility management systems.

- **Data Analytics:** Advanced analytics platforms process data from IoT devices, providing insights for predictive maintenance, demand forecasting, and energy optimization.

- **Renewable Energy Integration:** IoT plays a crucial role in integrating renewable energy sources such as solar and wind into the grid.

3. Energy and Utilities IoT Applications:

- **Smart Grids:** IoT transforms traditional power grids into smart grids, allowing real-time monitoring and control of energy flow, reducing outages, and enhancing resource management.

- **Smart Meters:** IoT-enabled smart meters provide consumers with real-time energy usage data and enable utilities to implement demand response programs.

- **Renewable Energy Management:** IoT sensors and analytics optimize the integration of renewable energy sources, ensuring efficient use and grid stability.

- **Energy Distribution:** IoT devices monitor and control energy distribution, improving the reliability and quality of electricity supply.

- **Water and Gas Utilities:** IoT sensors enable remote monitoring of water and gas infrastructure, reducing leaks and resource wastage.

4. Challenges in Energy and Utilities IoT:

- **Cybersecurity:** Protecting critical energy infrastructure from cyberattacks is a top priority in IoT deployments.

- **Data Management:** Handling the massive volumes of data generated by IoT devices requires robust data management and storage solutions.

- **Interoperability:** Ensuring compatibility between diverse IoT devices and systems is essential for seamless utility management.

- **Regulatory Compliance:** Utilities must adhere to strict regulatory guidelines to ensure data privacy and security.

5. Future Trends in Energy and Utilities IoT:

- **Edge Computing:** Edge computing will enable real-time data processing at the edge of the grid, reducing latency and enhancing responsiveness.

- **AI and Machine Learning:** AI algorithms will provide more accurate predictions, enhancing grid stability and energy optimization.

- **Blockchain:** Blockchain may find applications in utility billing and peer-to-peer energy trading.

- **Electric Vehicle Integration:** IoT will play a pivotal role in managing the integration of electric vehicles into the grid.

Conclusion:

Energy and utilities IoT is revolutionizing the way we generate, distribute, and manage energy resources. Smart grids, smart meters, and renewable energy integration are just a few examples of how IoT technology is enhancing efficiency and sustainability in the sector. Challenges such as cybersecurity and data management must be addressed, but as technology continues to evolve, energy and utilities IoT will play an increasingly vital role in shaping the future of energy management and utility services, ultimately contributing to a more sustainable and reliable energy ecosystem.

CHAPTER 10

Edge and Fog Computing in IoT

The advent of the Internet of Things (IoT) has ushered in an era of unprecedented data generation and connectivity. To harness the full potential of IoT, traditional cloud computing models have evolved to include Edge and Fog computing. These innovative paradigms bring computation and data analysis closer to the data source, enabling real-time decision-making and addressing the challenges of latency, bandwidth, and data privacy. In this exploration, we delve into the world of Edge and Fog computing in IoT, their significance, key concepts, applications, challenges, and the transformative impact they have on IoT ecosystems and industries worldwide.

A. Edge Computing Architecture: Empowering IoT with Real-time Processing

Edge computing architecture is a pivotal component in the Internet of Things (IoT) ecosystem, revolutionizing data processing and analysis by bringing computational resources closer to data sources. This paradigm shift reduces latency, enhances real-time decision-making, and addresses bandwidth constraints. In this exploration, we delve into the intricacies of edge computing architecture, its significance, key components, advantages, and the transformative impact it has on IoT applications and industries.

1. Significance of Edge Computing Architecture:

- **Latency Reduction:** By processing data closer to the data source, edge computing significantly reduces the time it takes for data to travel to centralized cloud servers and back, making real-time responses feasible.

- **Bandwidth Efficiency:** Edge computing reduces the amount of data that needs to be transmitted to the cloud, conserving network bandwidth and reducing costs.

- **Data Privacy:** Edge computing allows sensitive data to be processed locally, enhancing data privacy and compliance with regulations.

- **Reliability:** In applications where network connectivity is intermittent or unreliable, edge computing ensures continued operation and data processing.

2. Key Components of Edge Computing Architecture:

- **Edge Devices:** These are the IoT devices and sensors that generate data and perform initial data preprocessing. They are equipped with processing power and storage capabilities.

- **Edge Servers:** These servers, located at the edge of the network, receive and process data from edge devices. They may run specialized software for data analysis and filtering.

- **Local Storage:** Edge computing architecture often includes local storage to temporarily store data before transmission or for local processing.

- **Connectivity:** High-speed, low-latency connections, such as Wi-Fi or 5G, enable communication between edge devices, edge servers, and the central cloud infrastructure.

- **Analytics Software:** Edge servers run analytics software to process data locally and extract meaningful insights.

3. Advantages of Edge Computing Architecture:

- **Real-time Response:** Edge computing enables instant decision-making, critical for applications like autonomous vehicles, industrial automation, and healthcare.

- **Reduced Data Transfer Costs:** Processing data locally reduces the amount of data that needs to be sent to the cloud, saving on bandwidth costs.

- **Improved Scalability:** Edge computing allows for distributed processing, making it easier to scale resources as needed.

- **Enhanced Privacy and Security:** Sensitive data can be

processed and stored locally, reducing exposure to external threats.

4. Applications of Edge Computing Architecture:

- **Autonomous Vehicles:** Edge computing enables real-time analysis of sensor data for autonomous navigation and collision avoidance.

- **Smart Cities:** Edge computing enhances traffic management, surveillance, and public safety applications in smart cities.

- **Manufacturing and Industry 4.0:** Edge computing supports predictive maintenance, quality control, and process optimization in manufacturing.

- **Healthcare:** Medical devices and wearables use edge computing for real-time patient monitoring and remote diagnostics.

- **Retail:** Edge computing powers inventory management, customer analytics, and personalized marketing in retail environments.

5. Challenges in Edge Computing Architecture:

- **Resource Constraints:** Edge devices may have limited processing power and memory, which can be a constraint for complex applications.

- **Management Complexity:** Distributed edge infrastructure requires efficient management and monitoring to ensure reliability.

- **Standardization:** Lack of standardized protocols and frameworks can hinder interoperability and adoption.

- **Security:** Securing distributed edge systems against cyber threats is a complex challenge.

Conclusion:

Edge computing architecture is a fundamental enabler of real-time processing and decision-making in IoT applications. By bringing computation closer to data sources, it addresses latency, bandwidth, and data privacy concerns, unlocking the full potential of IoT across various industries. Challenges such as resource constraints and security must be tackled, but as technology advances, edge computing will continue to play a pivotal role in shaping the future of IoT applications and services.

B. Fog Computing Concepts: Bridging the Gap Between Cloud and Edge

Fog computing is a critical paradigm in the Internet of Things (IoT) landscape that extends the capabilities of edge computing by introducing intermediate computing layers between edge devices and centralized cloud data centers. It addresses the limitations of edge devices while providing lower latency and efficient data processing. In this exploration, we delve into the intricacies of fog computing concepts, their significance, key components, advantages, and the transformative impact they have on IoT applications and industries.

1. Significance of Fog Computing Concepts:

- **Latency Reduction:** Fog computing significantly reduces data transfer latency by processing data closer to edge devices, making real-time applications feasible.

- **Efficient Data Processing:** Fog nodes can perform data preprocessing, filtering, and analytics, reducing the volume of data that needs to be sent to the cloud.

- **Scalability:** Fog computing extends the capabilities of edge devices, allowing them to handle more complex tasks and scale resources as needed.

- **Reliability:** Fog nodes can provide redundancy and fault tolerance, ensuring continuous operation even in the event of device or network failures.

2. Key Components of Fog Computing Concepts:

- **Fog Nodes:** These are intermediate computing devices located between edge devices and cloud data centers. Fog nodes have processing power and storage capacity, enabling data processing and analysis.

- **Edge Devices:** Sensors, IoT devices, and endpoints that generate data and feed it into the fog computing environment.

- **Fog Networking:** High-speed, low-latency network connections connect edge devices to fog nodes and fog nodes to the cloud infrastructure.

- **Fog Analytics:** Specialized software and algorithms run on fog nodes to process and analyze data locally, extracting meaningful insights.

- **Orchestration and Management:** Fog computing requires tools for managing and orchestrating the deployment of fog nodes and their resources.

3. Advantages of Fog Computing Concepts:

- **Lower Latency:** Fog computing reduces data transfer times, making it suitable for applications requiring real-time responses, such as autonomous vehicles and industrial automation.

- **Efficient Data Usage:** By processing data locally, fog computing minimizes the amount of data sent to the cloud, reducing bandwidth costs and congestion.

- **Improved Scalability:** Fog nodes can be added or removed to match resource demands, making fog computing highly scalable.

- **Enhanced Reliability:** Redundancy and fault tolerance mechanisms in fog computing ensure reliable operation even in challenging network conditions.

4. Applications of Fog Computing Concepts:

- **Smart Grids:** Fog computing enhances grid management, optimizing energy distribution and enabling real-time response to grid events.

- **Healthcare:** Fog computing supports remote patient monitoring and telemedicine applications, improving healthcare delivery.

- **Autonomous Vehicles:** Fog computing enables real-time analysis of sensor data for autonomous navigation and safety.

- **Retail:** Inventory management, customer analytics, and personalized marketing benefit from the real-time processing capabilities of fog computing.

- **Manufacturing:** Fog computing supports predictive maintenance, process optimization, and quality control in manufacturing environments.

5. Challenges in Fog Computing Concepts:

- **Resource Allocation:** Efficiently distributing resources among fog nodes and managing their utilization can be complex.

- **Security:** Fog nodes must be secured against cyber threats, and data privacy concerns must be addressed.

- **Standardization:** Fog computing standards and protocols are still evolving, which can lead to interoperability challenges.

Conclusion:

Fog computing concepts bridge the gap between edge devices and centralized cloud data centers, offering lower latency, efficient data processing, and improved scalability. It is a critical enabler of real-time IoT applications across various industries. Challenges such as resource allocation and security must be tackled, but as technology advances and fog computing standards mature, it will continue to play a pivotal role in shaping the future of IoT applications and services.

C. Edge AI and Machine Learning: Powering Intelligent IoT Devices

Edge artificial intelligence (AI) and machine learning (ML) represent a groundbreaking convergence of IoT and AI technologies. By bringing AI and ML algorithms to the edge of the network, closer to data sources, these paradigms enable real-time processing, decision-making, and automation, transforming the capabilities of IoT devices. In this exploration, we delve into the intricacies of edge AI and machine learning, their significance, key components, applications, challenges, and the transformative impact they have on IoT ecosystems and industries.

1. Significance of Edge AI and Machine Learning:

- **Real-time Decision-Making:** Edge AI and ML enable IoT devices to make intelligent decisions locally, reducing latency and enhancing responsiveness in critical applications.

- **Bandwidth Efficiency:** Processing data at the edge reduces the need to transmit large volumes of data to centralized cloud servers, conserving network bandwidth.

- **Privacy and Data Security:** Local processing ensures that sensitive data remains on the device, enhancing privacy and security.

- **Resource Optimization:** Edge AI and ML can optimize resource usage, such as power, memory, and storage, making IoT devices more efficient.

2. Key Components of Edge AI and Machine Learning:

- **Edge Devices:** IoT devices equipped with processing

capabilities and sensors serve as the foundation for edge AI and ML.

- **Edge AI Chips:** Specialized hardware, including AI accelerators and neural processing units (NPUs), enable efficient execution of AI algorithms on edge devices.

- **Edge AI Software:** Lightweight AI and ML models optimized for edge devices, as well as inference engines, enable local processing.

- **Edge AI Frameworks:** Frameworks such as TensorFlow Lite and ONNX Runtime provide tools for developing and deploying edge AI and ML models.

- **Data Preprocessing:** Data preprocessing pipelines may include data cleaning, feature extraction, and normalization before feeding data to AI models.

3. Advantages of Edge AI and Machine Learning:

- **Low Latency:** Real-time processing on edge devices reduces response times, critical for applications like autonomous vehicles and industrial automation.

- **Privacy:** Sensitive data can be processed locally, minimizing the risk of data breaches and ensuring data privacy.

- **Bandwidth Savings:** Edge processing reduces the amount of data transmitted to the cloud, saving on network bandwidth and costs.

- **Offline Operation:** Edge AI devices can operate without continuous network connectivity, making them suitable for remote and isolated environments.

4. Applications of Edge AI and Machine Learning:

- **Autonomous Vehicles:** Edge AI processes sensor data for real-time decision-making in autonomous cars, ensuring safety and navigation.

- **Industrial IoT:** Edge ML optimizes manufacturing processes, predictive maintenance, and quality control in industrial settings.

- **Healthcare:** Edge AI supports remote patient monitoring, disease detection, and medical image analysis.

- **Smart Cameras:** Surveillance cameras equipped with edge AI can identify objects, individuals, and anomalies in real-time.

- **Agriculture:** Edge ML assists in crop monitoring, pest detection, and precision agriculture.

5. Challenges in Edge AI and Machine Learning:

- **Resource Constraints:** Edge devices often have limited

processing power and memory, challenging the deployment of complex AI models.

- **Model Training:** Training AI models typically requires substantial computational resources, which may not be available at the edge.

- **Security:** Securing edge AI devices against cyber threats is essential, especially when handling sensitive data.

- **Standardization:** Standardizing edge AI frameworks and interfaces can promote interoperability and simplify development.

Conclusion:

Edge AI and machine learning bring intelligence to IoT devices, enabling real-time decision-making, enhancing privacy, and conserving network bandwidth. While resource constraints and security challenges exist, technological advancements are driving the adoption of edge AI across various industries. As edge AI and ML continue to evolve, they will play an increasingly pivotal role in shaping the future of IoT applications and services, enabling a new era of intelligent and responsive devices.

D. Real-time Processing at the Edge: Enabling Instant Decision-Making in IoT

Real-time processing at the edge is a critical component of the Internet of Things (IoT) ecosystem that empowers IoT devices to make instant decisions and respond to events without relying on centralized cloud servers. By moving data processing closer to the data source, this paradigm minimizes latency and enhances responsiveness, making it ideal for applications that require immediate action. In this exploration, we delve into the intricacies of real-time processing at the edge, its significance, key components, advantages, applications, challenges, and the transformative impact it has on IoT ecosystems and industries.

1. Significance of Real-time Processing at the Edge:

- **Latency Reduction:** Edge computing significantly reduces data transfer times, making it suitable for applications that demand real-time responses, such as autonomous vehicles and industrial automation.

- **Instant Decision-Making:** Processing data at the edge allows IoT devices to make instantaneous decisions without relying on cloud-based services, enabling rapid response to critical events.

- **Bandwidth Efficiency:** By processing data locally, edge computing reduces the volume of data that needs to be transmitted to centralized cloud servers, conserving network bandwidth and reducing costs.

- **Resilience:** Edge devices can continue to operate even when network connectivity is lost, ensuring uninterrupted functionality in remote or intermittent connectivity scenarios.

2. Key Components of Real-time Processing at the Edge:

- **Edge Devices:** These are IoT devices equipped with processing capabilities and sensors, serving as the front line for data collection and processing.

- **Edge Servers:** Intermediate computing nodes, sometimes referred to as fog nodes, located closer to edge devices. They perform data preprocessing and analysis.

- **Low-Latency Networks:** High-speed, low-latency communication networks, such as 5G or Wi-Fi, connect edge devices to edge servers and the broader IoT ecosystem.

- **Real-time Analytics Software:** Specialized software and algorithms run on edge servers for real-time data processing, decision-making, and automation.

- **Local Storage:** Edge servers may include local storage for caching and storing data before transmission or for offline processing.

3. Advantages of Real-time Processing at the Edge:

- **Instantaneous Response:** Real-time processing enables instant decision-making, critical for applications like autonomous vehicles and industrial control systems.

- **Privacy and Data Security:** Processing data locally enhances data privacy and security by reducing the need to transmit sensitive information to the cloud.

- **Resource Optimization:** Edge devices can optimize resource usage, such as power, memory, and storage, making IoT devices more efficient.

- **Offline Operation:** Edge devices can continue to operate independently, even when network connectivity is lost, ensuring continued functionality.

4. Applications of Real-time Processing at the Edge:

- **Autonomous Vehicles:** Real-time edge processing is crucial for processing sensor data and enabling instant decision-making in self-driving cars.

- **Industrial IoT:** It supports real-time control and automation of manufacturing processes, predictive maintenance, and quality control in industrial environments.

- **Healthcare:** Real-time monitoring and diagnostics in

healthcare devices, such as patient monitors and wearable health trackers.

- **Smart Cities:** Real-time processing enhances traffic management, surveillance, and public safety applications in smart city deployments.

- **Retail:** Inventory management, customer analytics, and personalized marketing benefit from real-time processing capabilities.

5. Challenges in Real-time Processing at the Edge:

- **Resource Constraints:** Edge devices often have limited processing power and memory, challenging the deployment of complex real-time applications.

- **Security:** Securing edge devices and edge servers against cyber threats is crucial, especially when handling sensitive data.

- **Interoperability:** Ensuring compatibility between diverse edge devices and edge servers can be challenging.

- **Scalability:** Managing and scaling edge infrastructure efficiently is a complex task.

Conclusion:

Real-time processing at the edge empowers IoT devices to

make instant decisions and respond rapidly to events. By reducing latency, enhancing privacy, and conserving network bandwidth, this paradigm has a transformative impact on IoT applications across various industries. Challenges like resource constraints and security must be addressed, but as technology advances, real-time processing at the edge will continue to play a pivotal role in shaping the future of IoT ecosystems and services, enabling a new era of responsive and intelligent devices.

E. Use Cases for Edge and Fog Computing: Transforming Industries with Distributed Intelligence

Edge and fog computing, by bringing computational capabilities closer to the data source, have revolutionized various industries by enabling real-time processing, low latency, and efficient data analysis. These paradigms empower IoT devices to make quicker decisions, enhance privacy, and reduce bandwidth usage. In this exploration, we delve into the diverse use cases for edge and fog computing across industries, showcasing how these technologies are transforming the way we work and live.

1. Autonomous Vehicles:

- *Real-time Decision-Making:* Edge and fog computing enable autonomous vehicles to process sensor data instantly, ensuring rapid responses to changing road conditions and potential hazards.

- *Enhanced Safety:* These technologies support collision avoidance, adaptive cruise control, and traffic management systems, enhancing road safety.

- *Data Privacy:* Local processing ensures that sensitive vehicle data, such as driver behavior or navigation routes, remains on the vehicle, preserving user privacy.

2. Industrial IoT (IIoT):

- *Predictive Maintenance:* Edge and fog computing analyze sensor data from machinery and equipment, predicting maintenance needs and reducing downtime.

- *Quality Control:* Real-time monitoring and analysis of production processes improve product quality and reduce defects.

- *Energy Management:* IIoT systems optimize energy usage in factories, reducing costs and environmental impact.

3. Healthcare:

- *Remote Patient Monitoring:* Edge and fog computing enable real-time monitoring of patient health data, allowing healthcare providers to respond quickly to critical situations.

- *Medical Imaging:* Local processing enhances medical

imaging devices' ability to analyze and diagnose medical conditions.

- *Wearable Health Devices:* These technologies support wearable devices that monitor vital signs, providing valuable health insights to users and healthcare professionals.

4. Smart Cities:

- *Traffic Management:* Edge and fog computing optimize traffic flow, reduce congestion, and enhance road safety through real-time analysis of traffic data.

- *Public Safety:* Surveillance cameras with edge processing can identify security threats and suspicious activities in real-time.

- *Environmental Monitoring:* These technologies assist in monitoring air quality, weather conditions, and pollution levels for better environmental management.

5. Retail:

- *Inventory Management:* Edge and fog computing enhance inventory control through real-time tracking and analytics, reducing stockouts and overstock situations.

- *Customer Analytics:* Real-time data analysis enables personalized marketing, dynamic pricing, and improved customer experiences.

- *Loss Prevention:* Surveillance systems with edge processing can detect theft and fraud in real-time.

6. Agriculture:

- *Crop Monitoring:* Edge and fog computing support remote monitoring of crops, enabling farmers to optimize irrigation, detect diseases, and improve yield.

- *Precision Agriculture:* These technologies assist in precise application of fertilizers, pesticides, and water resources.

- *Livestock Monitoring:* Real-time data from sensors on livestock can help manage animal health and productivity.

7. Energy Management:

- *Smart Grids:* Edge and fog computing optimize energy distribution, manage renewable energy sources, and enhance grid resilience.

- *Energy Consumption Analysis:* Real-time analysis of energy usage data helps consumers and businesses optimize their power consumption.

8. Environmental Monitoring:

- *Air and Water Quality Monitoring:* Edge and fog computing assist in real-time monitoring of air and water quality, enabling early detection of pollution and environmental hazards.

- *Natural Disaster Detection:* These technologies can analyze data from sensors to detect earthquakes, wildfires, and other natural disasters in real-time.

9. Retail:

- *Inventory Management:* Edge and fog computing enhance inventory control through real-time tracking and analytics, reducing stockouts and overstock situations.

- *Customer Analytics:* Real-time data analysis enables personalized marketing, dynamic pricing, and improved customer experiences.

- *Loss Prevention:* Surveillance systems with edge processing can detect theft and fraud in real-time.

10. Oil and Gas:

- *Remote Monitoring:* Edge and fog computing enable real-time monitoring of oil and gas infrastructure, enhancing safety and optimizing operations.

- *Predictive Maintenance:* These technologies predict equipment failures, reducing downtime and maintenance costs.

- *Environmental Compliance:* Real-time data analysis helps companies meet environmental regulations and mitigate environmental risks.

Conclusion:

Edge and fog computing have found applications across a wide range of industries, from autonomous vehicles to healthcare, agriculture, and environmental monitoring. By enabling real-time processing, low-latency responses, and data privacy, these technologies are transforming the way businesses operate and the services they provide. As edge and fog computing continue to advance, they will drive further innovation and efficiency in these industries, shaping the future of IoT and distributed intelligence.

CHAPTER 11

Advanced IoT Topics

As the Internet of Things (IoT) continues its rapid evolution, it delves into realms of innovation that push the boundaries of what's possible. Advanced IoT topics encompass a diverse array of subjects that incorporate emerging technologies, novel applications, and forward-looking concepts. In this exploration, we embark on a journey through these advanced IoT topics, exploring how they are reshaping industries, driving scientific discovery, and opening doors to a future limited only by our imagination. From blockchain's influence on IoT to the potential of quantum computing and the fusion of AI, this is a glimpse into the frontiers of IoT innovation.

A. Blockchain and IoT: Securing the Future of Connectivity

Blockchain technology, known for its decentralized, secure, and transparent nature, has found a powerful ally in the Internet of Things (IoT). The convergence of these two technologies promises to revolutionize the way data is collected, stored, and shared in IoT ecosystems. In this exploration, we delve into the intricate relationship between blockchain and IoT, uncovering their significance, key components, advantages, challenges, and the transformative impact they have on data security, trust, and the future of interconnected devices.

1. Significance of Blockchain in IoT:

- **Enhanced Security:** Blockchain's immutable and tamper-proof ledger provides robust protection against unauthorized access and data breaches, making IoT data more secure.

- **Data Integrity:** The transparent and decentralized nature of blockchain ensures the integrity of IoT data, reducing the risk of data manipulation or fraud.

- **Trust and Transparency:** Blockchain enables trust between parties in IoT transactions, eliminating the need for intermediaries and reducing costs.

- **Smart Contracts:** Smart contracts, self-executing code on the blockchain, automate and secure IoT transactions, facilitating seamless, trustless interactions.

2. Key Components of Blockchain in IoT:

- **Blockchain Networks:** Private, public, or consortium blockchains can be used to secure IoT data and transactions.

- **IoT Devices:** Sensors, actuators, and edge devices generate data that is recorded on the blockchain.

- **Decentralized Consensus:** Various consensus mechanisms, such as Proof of Work (PoW) or Proof of Stake (PoS), ensure agreement on the state of the blockchain.

- **Smart Contracts:** Self-executing code on the blockchain automates IoT transactions, reducing the need for intermediaries.

- **Immutable Ledger:** Data on the blockchain cannot be altered or deleted, ensuring data integrity.

3. Advantages of Blockchain in IoT:

- **Security:** Blockchain's cryptographic features protect IoT data from unauthorized access and tampering.

- **Data Integrity:** The decentralized ledger guarantees the integrity and accuracy of IoT data.

- **Interoperability:** Blockchain standardizes and simplifies data exchange among different IoT devices and platforms.

- **Efficiency:** Smart contracts automate processes, reducing the need for intermediaries and streamlining transactions.

4. Applications of Blockchain in IoT:

- **Supply Chain Management:** Blockchain ensures the transparency and traceability of goods in the supply chain, reducing fraud and improving efficiency.

- **Smart Contracts in IoT:** Self-executing smart contracts enable automated, secure, and transparent interactions between IoT devices.

- **IoT Security:** Blockchain enhances the security of IoT devices, making them less susceptible to cyberattacks.

- **Asset Tracking:** Industries like logistics and transportation use blockchain to track assets in real-time.

- **Energy Trading:** Blockchain facilitates peer-to-peer energy trading among IoT-enabled renewable energy sources.

5. Challenges in Blockchain in IoT:

- **Scalability:** Blockchain networks must handle the vast amount of data generated by IoT devices, posing scalability challenges.

- **Complexity:** Integrating blockchain with existing IoT infrastructure can be complex and resource-intensive.

- **Energy Consumption:** Some blockchain consensus mechanisms, like PoW, are energy-intensive, which may not be sustainable for IoT devices.

- **Standardization:** Lack of standardized protocols and interoperability can hinder adoption.

Conclusion:

Blockchain and IoT form a powerful alliance, promising heightened security, trust, and transparency in the interconnected world of devices. Despite challenges, the potential for blockchain in IoT is vast, offering opportunities for innovation across industries. As these technologies continue to mature and find wider acceptance, they will shape the future of data security, automation, and trust in our increasingly connected world.

B. Quantum Computing and IoT: A Quantum Leap into the Future of Connectivity

The integration of quantum computing and the Internet of Things (IoT) represents a remarkable convergence of cutting-edge technologies. Quantum computing holds the promise of performing complex calculations at speeds that were previously unimaginable, and when coupled with IoT, it can transform the capabilities of connected devices. In this exploration, we delve into the profound relationship between quantum computing and IoT, uncovering their significance, key components, advantages, challenges, and the transformative impact they have on data processing, security, and the future of interconnected devices.

1. Significance of Quantum Computing in IoT:

- **Unprecedented Computational Power:** Quantum computers

have the potential to solve problems that are currently intractable for classical computers, significantly enhancing the capabilities of IoT devices.

- **Enhanced Data Processing:** Quantum computing enables rapid analysis of vast datasets generated by IoT devices, supporting real-time decision-making and insights.

- **Stronger Security:** Quantum-resistant cryptographic algorithms can secure IoT data from future quantum attacks, ensuring data integrity and privacy.

- **Optimized Resource Management:** Quantum algorithms can optimize resource allocation and energy usage in IoT networks, improving efficiency.

2. Key Components of Quantum Computing in IoT:

- **Quantum Computers:** Specialized quantum processors capable of performing quantum computations.

- **Quantum Algorithms:** Algorithms designed to harness the computational power of quantum computers for tasks such as optimization, machine learning, and encryption.

- **IoT Devices:** Sensors, actuators, and edge devices that generate data and interact with the physical world.

- **Quantum-Enabled Communication:** Quantum key

distribution (QKD) and quantum-resistant cryptography ensure secure communication between IoT devices.

- **Quantum Simulators:** Quantum simulators mimic quantum behavior to model and optimize IoT systems.

3. Advantages of Quantum Computing in IoT:

- **Speed:** Quantum computers can process data at speeds exponentially faster than classical computers, enabling real-time analysis of IoT data.

- **Security:** Quantum-resistant cryptographic algorithms protect IoT data from future quantum attacks, enhancing security.

- **Resource Optimization:** Quantum algorithms can optimize resource allocation in IoT networks, reducing energy consumption and costs.

- **Advanced Machine Learning:** Quantum machine learning algorithms can extract deeper insights from IoT data, improving predictive capabilities.

4. Applications of Quantum Computing in IoT:

- **Optimized Supply Chain:** Quantum computing can optimize supply chain logistics, reducing inefficiencies and costs.

- **Quantum Machine Learning:** IoT devices equipped with quantum machine learning can provide more accurate predictions and recommendations.

- **Secure IoT Communications:** Quantum-resistant cryptography ensures secure communication between IoT devices, safeguarding data privacy.

- **Energy Efficiency:** Quantum algorithms can optimize energy usage in IoT networks, extending the lifespan of battery-powered devices.

5. Challenges in Quantum Computing in IoT:

- **Technology Maturity:** Quantum computing is still in its infancy, with practical quantum computers limited in availability and scalability.

- **Integration Complexity:** Integrating quantum computing with existing IoT infrastructure can be challenging and resource-intensive.

- **Quantum-Ready Hardware:** IoT devices need to be quantum-ready to leverage the benefits of quantum computing fully.

- **Energy Consumption:** Quantum computers are currently energy-intensive, which may pose challenges for battery-powered IoT devices.

Conclusion:

Quantum computing and IoT represent a formidable alliance with the potential to revolutionize data processing, security, and efficiency in the interconnected world of devices. Although challenges exist, the future holds promise as both quantum computing and IoT technologies continue to advance. Their convergence will unlock new realms of possibility, enabling more powerful, secure, and efficient IoT ecosystems that can shape the future of technology and connectivity.

C. AI and Machine Learning in IoT: Unlocking the Power of Data

The synergy between Artificial Intelligence (AI), Machine Learning (ML), and the Internet of Things (IoT) is transforming the way data is collected, analyzed, and acted upon in various domains. AI and ML empower IoT devices to make intelligent decisions, predict outcomes, and automate processes, thereby enhancing efficiency, accuracy, and insights. In this exploration, we delve into the intricate relationship between AI, ML, and IoT, uncovering their significance, key components, advantages, challenges, and the transformative impact they have on data-driven decision-making, predictive analytics, and the future of interconnected devices.

1. Significance of AI and Machine Learning in IoT:

- **Data Analysis and Insights:** AI and ML enable IoT devices to analyze vast datasets in real-time, extracting valuable insights and patterns.

- **Predictive Analytics:** ML models can forecast future events, enabling proactive decision-making and preventive maintenance.

- **Automation:** AI-powered IoT devices can automate routine tasks, reducing human intervention and increasing efficiency.

- **Adaptability:** ML algorithms can adapt and optimize device behavior based on changing conditions, improving performance.

2. Key Components of AI and Machine Learning in IoT:

- **IoT Devices:** Sensors, actuators, and edge devices equipped with data collection and processing capabilities.

- **AI/ML Models:** Machine learning models, including supervised, unsupervised, and reinforcement learning, trained to perform specific tasks.

- **Data Processing Platforms:** Cloud-based or edge-based platforms that preprocess, store, and analyze IoT data.

- **Real-time Analytics:** Algorithms that process data in real-time, enabling immediate decision-making.

- **Feedback Loops:** Systems that use AI-generated insights to optimize device behavior and performance.

3. Advantages of AI and Machine Learning in IoT:

- **Data-Driven Decisions:** AI and ML provide data-driven insights, improving the quality of decision-making.

- **Predictive Maintenance:** ML models can predict when equipment or devices will require maintenance, reducing downtime and costs.

- **Energy Efficiency:** AI can optimize resource usage, such as power and bandwidth, in IoT networks, extending device lifespan.

- **Enhanced Security:** AI-based anomaly detection can identify security threats and breaches in real-time.

4. Applications of AI and Machine Learning in IoT:

- **Smart Cities:** AI-driven traffic management, energy optimization, and public safety applications improve urban living.

- **Healthcare:** Remote patient monitoring, predictive diagnostics, and drug discovery benefit from AI and ML insights.

- **Manufacturing:** Predictive maintenance, quality control, and process optimization enhance manufacturing efficiency.

- **Agriculture:** ML models optimize irrigation, crop monitoring, and pest control in precision agriculture.

- **Retail:** AI-driven inventory management, customer analytics, and personalized marketing enhance the retail experience.

5. Challenges in AI and Machine Learning in IoT:

- **Data Privacy:** Handling sensitive IoT data requires robust privacy measures and compliance with regulations.

- **Scalability:** Managing and processing vast amounts of IoT data can strain existing infrastructure.

- **Interoperability:** Ensuring compatibility between diverse IoT devices and AI/ML models can be challenging.

- **Algorithm Transparency:** Understanding and explaining AI/ML model decisions is crucial for trust and accountability.

Conclusion:

AI and Machine Learning have breathed new life into IoT, making it smarter, more efficient, and predictive. The convergence of these technologies enhances decision-making, automates processes, and extracts valuable insights from the deluge of IoT data. While challenges such as data privacy and scalability remain, the future promises even greater advancements in AI and ML for IoT, ultimately reshaping industries and offering a glimpse into a more connected, intelligent, and data-driven world.

D. IoT in Space and Satellite Communication: Bridging Earth and Beyond

The application of the Internet of Things (IoT) in space and satellite communication represents a significant leap in the evolution of space technology. It enables the seamless integration of data from satellites, space probes, and ground-based systems, fostering improved communication, monitoring, and exploration of space. In this exploration, we delve into the intricate relationship between IoT and space technology, uncovering their significance, key components, advantages, challenges, and the transformative impact they have on space exploration, satellite communication, and our understanding of the cosmos.

1. Significance of IoT in Space and Satellite Communication:

- **Data Collection and Transmission:** IoT-enabled sensors and devices in space gather and transmit data from remote celestial bodies, enabling real-time monitoring and research.

- **Enhanced Satellite Communication:** IoT technology

improves satellite communication systems, enhancing data transmission and enabling global coverage.

- **Space Exploration:** IoT devices on space probes and rovers provide vital information for planetary exploration and scientific research.

- **Remote Sensing:** IoT-equipped satellites monitor Earth's climate, weather, and natural disasters, aiding in disaster management and environmental research.

2. Key Components of IoT in Space and Satellite Communication:

- **Spaceborne IoT Devices:** Sensors, cameras, and communication equipment aboard satellites, space probes, and the International Space Station (ISS).

- **Ground Stations:** Earth-based stations receive and transmit data to and from spaceborne IoT devices.

- **Satellite Networks:** Constellations of interconnected satellites form the backbone of space-based IoT communication.

- **IoT Protocols:** Specialized communication protocols designed for space IoT applications, ensuring data integrity and reliability.

- **Data Centers:** Large data centers process and analyze the vast amount of data generated by space IoT devices.

3. Advantages of IoT in Space and Satellite Communication:

- **Global Connectivity:** IoT-enabled satellites provide worldwide connectivity, bridging remote areas and enhancing communication in underserved regions.

- **Real-time Data:** IoT devices in space offer real-time data collection and transmission, critical for applications such as weather forecasting and disaster management.

- **Space Exploration:** IoT-equipped space probes and rovers transmit valuable scientific data from distant celestial bodies, advancing our understanding of the cosmos.

- **Environmental Monitoring:** IoT-enabled satellites monitor Earth's climate, weather, and natural disasters, contributing to environmental research and disaster preparedness.

4. Applications of IoT in Space and Satellite Communication:

- **Navigation and Positioning:** GPS satellites, equipped with IoT technology, provide precise location data for navigation and geolocation services.

- **Earth Observation:** IoT-equipped satellites monitor Earth's climate, weather patterns, and environmental changes, aiding in agriculture, forestry, and disaster management.

- **Space Exploration:** Space probes and rovers equipped with IoT devices explore planets, moons, and asteroids, sending back invaluable data.

- **Global Internet Coverage:** Low Earth Orbit (LEO) satellite constellations, such as those by SpaceX's Starlink and OneWeb, aim to provide global internet coverage through IoT technology.

5. Challenges in IoT in Space and Satellite Communication:

- **Data Security:** Ensuring the security and encryption of IoT data transmitted between space and Earth is crucial to prevent unauthorized access.

- **Space Debris:** The increasing number of satellites in orbit raises concerns about space debris and collisions, posing a threat to existing infrastructure.

- **Cost and Complexity:** Developing, launching, and maintaining spaceborne IoT devices and satellite constellations is costly and complex.

- **Spectrum Allocation:** Ensuring sufficient radio spectrum for IoT satellite communication without interference is a regulatory challenge.

Conclusion:

IoT technology in space and satellite communication is opening up new frontiers in space exploration, communication, and Earth monitoring. As technology continues to advance, we can expect even greater connectivity, data transmission, and insights from the cosmos. While challenges such as data security and space debris management persist, the fusion of IoT and space technology holds the potential to revolutionize our understanding of the universe and provide unprecedented global connectivity and communication capabilities.

E. Ethical and Sustainable IoT: Navigating the Digital Frontier Responsibly

The Internet of Things (IoT), with its vast network of interconnected devices, presents unique ethical and sustainability challenges that need careful consideration. As IoT continues to expand its influence in various domains, it's essential to ensure that its growth aligns with ethical principles and contributes to a sustainable future. In this exploration, we delve into the ethical and sustainability dimensions of IoT, uncovering their significance, key principles, challenges, and the transformative impact they can have on shaping a responsible digital future.

1. Significance of Ethical and Sustainable IoT:

- **Data Privacy:** Ethical IoT practices ensure the protection of users' sensitive data, fostering trust and compliance with privacy regulations.

- **Resource Efficiency:** Sustainable IoT designs reduce energy consumption, extend device lifespan, and minimize electronic waste, contributing to environmental goals.

- **Digital Inclusion:** Ethical IoT aims to bridge the digital divide, ensuring equal access and opportunities for all individuals and communities.

- **Responsible AI:** Ethical considerations in AI, often intertwined with IoT, help prevent bias, discrimination, and misuse of AI algorithms.

2. Key Principles of Ethical and Sustainable IoT:

- **Privacy by Design:** IoT systems should incorporate privacy protections from the outset, limiting data collection to what is necessary and providing users with control over their data.

- **Transparency:** IoT providers should be transparent about data collection, usage, and sharing practices, fostering trust among users.

- **Data Security:** Robust security measures should safeguard

IoT data from breaches and cyberattacks, ensuring data integrity and user safety.

- **Resource Efficiency:** Sustainable IoT designs should prioritize energy efficiency, reduce electronic waste, and promote device recycling.

- **Accessibility:** IoT systems should be accessible to people with disabilities, ensuring inclusivity.

3. Advantages of Ethical and Sustainable IoT:

- **Trust and Adoption:** Ethical practices build trust with users, increasing IoT adoption and user engagement.

- **Environmental Impact:** Sustainable IoT reduces energy consumption and electronic waste, contributing to a greener future.

- **Social Impact:** Ethical IoT aims to address societal challenges, such as healthcare, mobility, and accessibility, improving quality of life.

- **Long-Term Viability:** Sustainable practices ensure the long-term viability of IoT technologies by minimizing their environmental footprint.

4. Challenges in Ethical and Sustainable IoT:

- **Data Privacy:** Balancing data collection for legitimate purposes with privacy concerns is a complex ethical challenge.

- **Security:** IoT devices are vulnerable to cyberattacks, and securing them while maintaining user privacy is a delicate balance.

- **Resource Constraints:** Achieving sustainability in IoT may require additional investments in energy-efficient hardware and infrastructure.

- **Regulatory Compliance:** Keeping up with evolving data privacy and environmental regulations is challenging for IoT providers.

5. Applications of Ethical and Sustainable IoT:

- **Healthcare:** Ethical IoT ensures the privacy and security of patient data in remote health monitoring and telemedicine applications.

- **Smart Cities:** Sustainable IoT technologies optimize resource usage in urban environments, reducing energy consumption and emissions.

- **Agriculture:** Ethical and sustainable IoT practices improve crop monitoring and precision agriculture while minimizing resource waste.

- **Wearable Technology:** IoT wearables focus on user privacy and energy efficiency while delivering valuable health insights.

Conclusion:

Ethical and sustainable IoT practices are essential for navigating the digital frontier responsibly. As IoT continues to transform industries and daily life, the adoption of ethical principles and sustainability measures becomes paramount. Balancing innovation with responsibility ensures that IoT not only enhances our lives but also contributes to a better, more equitable, and environmentally conscious future. By addressing the ethical and sustainability dimensions of IoT, we can harness its full potential while safeguarding the interests of individuals, society, and the planet.

CHAPTER 12

Future Trends in IoT

The Internet of Things (IoT) has been a driving force behind digital transformation, revolutionizing industries and reshaping the way we live and work. Yet, as IoT continues to mature, it embarks on a journey into an even more dynamic and transformative future. In this exploration, we gaze into the crystal ball of technology to uncover the emerging trends that are poised to define the next phase of IoT evolution. From the integration of edge AI to the impact of quantum computing and the proliferation of IoT in healthcare, these trends promise to reshape industries, create new possibilities, and chart a course toward an even more connected, intelligent, and data-driven world.

A. Edge AI and IoT: The Convergence of Intelligence at the Fringe

The convergence of Edge Artificial Intelligence (AI) and the Internet of Things (IoT) represents a transformative force that is revolutionizing the way we process data, make decisions, and interact with the digital world. Edge AI brings machine learning and intelligent processing closer to the data source, enabling real-time analysis, faster response times, and reduced reliance on centralized cloud infrastructure. In this exploration, we delve into the intricate relationship between Edge AI and IoT, uncovering their significance, key components, advantages, challenges, and the transformative impact they have on data processing, device autonomy, and the future of connected systems.

1. Significance of Edge AI and IoT:

- **Real-time Decision-Making:** Edge AI enables IoT devices to make intelligent decisions locally, reducing latency and improving responsiveness.

- **Data Privacy:** Edge AI processes sensitive data on the device, reducing the need to transmit it to the cloud, enhancing privacy and security.

- **Scalability:** Distributing AI processing to edge devices enables more efficient scaling of IoT deployments.

- **Autonomous Devices:** Edge AI empowers IoT devices to act autonomously, reducing dependence on centralized controllers.

2. Key Components of Edge AI and IoT:

- **IoT Devices:** Sensors, cameras, and edge devices equipped with data collection and processing capabilities.

- **Edge Servers:** Local computing resources, often integrated into edge devices or nearby infrastructure, perform AI inference and data processing.

- **AI Models:** Machine learning models designed for efficient execution on resource-constrained edge devices.

- **Connectivity:** Wired or wireless connections enable communication between edge devices and central systems when necessary.

- **Data Storage:** Edge devices may have limited storage capacity, necessitating data offloading to centralized storage when needed.

3. Advantages of Edge AI and IoT:

- **Reduced Latency:** Processing data at the edge reduces latency, making real-time decision-making possible.

- **Privacy and Security:** Edge AI limits data transmission to the cloud, reducing the exposure of sensitive information.

- **Efficiency:** Edge AI optimizes resource usage, reducing bandwidth consumption and cloud processing costs.

- **Offline Operation:** Edge AI allows devices to operate independently of continuous cloud connectivity.

4. Applications of Edge AI and IoT:

- **Smart Cities:** Edge AI and IoT enable real-time traffic management, video analytics, and environmental monitoring.

- **Manufacturing:** Edge AI improves quality control, predictive maintenance, and process optimization in smart factories.

- **Healthcare:** IoT devices with Edge AI capabilities enable remote patient monitoring, diagnosis, and personalized treatment.

- **Autonomous Vehicles:** Edge AI powers decision-making in self-driving cars, enhancing safety and reliability.

- **Retail:** Edge AI supports cashier-less stores, inventory management, and personalized shopping experiences.

5. Challenges in Edge AI and IoT:

- **Resource Constraints:** Edge devices may have limited computing power, memory, and energy, posing challenges for AI model execution.

- **Model Size:** Efficient AI models must be developed to fit on resource-constrained edge devices.

- **Data Synchronization:** Ensuring data consistency and synchronization across edge devices and central systems can be complex.

- **Security:** Securing edge devices against physical and cyber threats is essential.

Conclusion:

The convergence of Edge AI and IoT represents a paradigm shift in the way we process data and make decisions. This transformative technology promises to unlock new possibilities, from autonomous vehicles to more responsive and secure smart cities. As Edge AI and IoT continue to evolve, addressing challenges such as resource constraints and security will be critical to harnessing their full potential. The future of intelligent, data-driven systems lies at the edge, where real-time insights and autonomous decision-making are shaping a more connected and responsive world.

B. IoT in Healthcare Revolution: Transforming Patient Care and Beyond

The Internet of Things (IoT) is revolutionizing the healthcare industry by enhancing patient care, streamlining processes, and enabling innovative solutions. IoT devices and applications are driving the digitization of healthcare, offering real-time monitoring, remote patient management, and data-driven insights. In this exploration, we delve into the profound impact of IoT on healthcare, uncovering its significance, key components, advantages, challenges, and the transformative future it promises for patients, healthcare providers, and the industry as a whole.

1. Significance of IoT in Healthcare:

- **Remote Patient Monitoring:** IoT devices enable continuous, real-time monitoring of patients' vital signs, chronic conditions, and recovery progress, reducing hospitalization rates and improving patient outcomes.

- **Data-Driven Insights:** IoT generates vast amounts of healthcare data, which can be analyzed to identify trends, predict disease outbreaks, and personalize treatment plans.

- **Efficiency and Cost Reduction:** IoT streamlines healthcare processes, optimizing resource allocation, reducing administrative burdens, and lowering operational costs.

- **Improved Decision-Making:** Healthcare professionals gain access to real-time patient data, enhancing diagnostic accuracy and enabling faster treatment decisions.

2. Key Components of IoT in Healthcare:

- **IoT Devices:** Wearables, sensors, and medical devices collect patient data and transmit it to healthcare systems.

- **Connectivity:** Wired and wireless networks facilitate data transmission between devices, hospitals, and cloud platforms.

- **Data Analytics:** Advanced analytics and machine learning algorithms process and analyze healthcare data for actionable insights.

- **Electronic Health Records (EHRs):** Centralized electronic records store patient information, facilitating data sharing among healthcare providers.

- **Cloud Computing:** Scalable cloud platforms store and process vast amounts of healthcare data securely.

3. Advantages of IoT in Healthcare:

- **Early Disease Detection:** Continuous monitoring enables early detection of health issues, allowing for timely intervention.

- **Personalized Medicine:** IoT data enables the customization of treatment plans, medications, and interventions based on individual patient data.

- **Reduced Hospitalizations:** Remote monitoring and early intervention help reduce hospital admissions and readmissions.

- **Streamlined Workflow:** IoT optimizes healthcare processes, reducing administrative overhead and improving efficiency.

4. Applications of IoT in Healthcare:

- **Remote Patient Monitoring:** IoT devices track vital signs, chronic conditions, and post-surgery recovery remotely, keeping patients out of the hospital.

- **Telemedicine:** Virtual consultations and remote diagnostics leverage IoT for convenient and accessible healthcare.

- **Smart Hospitals:** IoT-enabled infrastructure optimizes resource allocation, enhances patient experience, and improves security.

- **Drug Management:** IoT devices help monitor medication adherence, reducing medication errors and improving patient compliance.

- **Predictive Analytics:** IoT data is used to predict disease outbreaks, enabling proactive public health measures.

5. Challenges in IoT in Healthcare:

- **Data Privacy:** Protecting sensitive patient data is a paramount concern, requiring robust security measures and compliance with regulations like HIPAA.

- **Interoperability:** Ensuring compatibility among diverse IoT devices and healthcare systems is essential for data sharing and integration.

- **Data Accuracy:** IoT devices must provide accurate data to support reliable clinical decision-making.

- **Regulatory Compliance:** Adhering to healthcare regulations and standards is a complex challenge.

Conclusion:

IoT is at the forefront of a healthcare revolution, offering new ways to monitor, diagnose, and treat patients. As technology continues to advance, the potential for IoT to transform healthcare is boundless. Overcoming challenges related to data privacy, interoperability, and accuracy will be crucial to realizing the full potential of IoT in healthcare. The future promises not only improved patient care but also more efficient and cost-effective healthcare systems that can benefit individuals and communities worldwide.

C. Quantum Computing and IoT Impact: Revolutionizing Data Processing

The synergy between quantum computing and the Internet of Things (IoT) promises to usher in a new era of computing capabilities, transforming how data is processed, encrypted, and communicated. Quantum computing, with its potential to perform complex calculations at speeds currently unimaginable, holds the key to solving computational problems that were previously unsolvable. In this exploration, we delve into the profound impact of quantum computing on IoT, uncovering its significance, key components, advantages, challenges, and the transformative future it holds for data-intensive applications and industries.

1. Significance of Quantum Computing in IoT:

- **Speed and Efficiency:** Quantum computers can perform complex calculations exponentially faster than classical computers, enabling real-time analysis of vast IoT datasets.

- **Cryptography and Security:** Quantum-resistant encryption techniques are vital as quantum computers could break existing encryption methods, making data security in IoT more robust.

- **Optimized Algorithms:** Quantum algorithms can optimize resource usage, routing, and data processing, improving the efficiency of IoT networks.

- **Simulation and Modeling:** Quantum computing enables precise simulation of physical systems, benefiting fields like materials science and climate modeling.

2. Key Components of Quantum Computing and IoT Impact:

- **Quantum Bits (Qubits):** The fundamental unit of quantum computing that can exist in multiple states simultaneously, enabling parallel processing.

- **Quantum Computers:** Specialized hardware designed to

manipulate qubits and perform quantum calculations.

- **Quantum Cryptography:** Novel cryptographic methods leveraging quantum properties for secure communication.

- **Quantum Algorithms:** Algorithms tailored for quantum computers to solve complex problems efficiently.

- **Quantum Sensors:** Sensitive quantum sensors can enhance data collection in IoT applications.

3. Advantages of Quantum Computing in IoT:

- **Real-time Analytics:** Quantum computing accelerates data analysis, allowing IoT devices to make faster, more informed decisions.

- **Secure Communication:** Quantum-resistant encryption ensures data security in IoT, even against quantum attacks.

- **Optimized Resource Usage:** Quantum algorithms can optimize IoT network routing and resource allocation, reducing energy consumption.

- **Innovative Applications:** Quantum computing enables the development of novel IoT applications in fields like healthcare, finance, and materials science.

4. Applications of Quantum Computing in IoT:

- **Optimized Routing:** Quantum algorithms can improve data routing in IoT networks, reducing latency and energy consumption.

- **Data Analytics:** Quantum computing accelerates data analysis, enabling real-time insights for IoT devices in fields like predictive maintenance and finance.

- **Secure IoT:** Quantum-resistant encryption ensures data security in IoT applications, protecting sensitive information.

- **Materials Discovery:** Quantum simulations aid in the discovery of new materials with applications in energy, electronics, and healthcare.

5. Challenges in Quantum Computing and IoT Impact:

- **Technology Maturity:** Quantum computing is still in its early stages, and practical, scalable quantum hardware is under development.

- **Integration Complexity:** Integrating quantum technology with existing IoT infrastructure poses technical and logistical challenges.

- **Data Security:** While quantum-resistant encryption is emerging, its implementation and adoption in IoT may take time.

- **Regulatory Compliance:** Addressing regulatory and compliance issues associated with quantum computing in IoT is a complex task.

Conclusion:

The marriage of quantum computing and IoT holds immense promise for revolutionizing data processing, security, and optimization. As quantum technology continues to advance, its integration into IoT ecosystems will become increasingly prevalent. Overcoming challenges related to technology maturity, integration complexity, and data security will be critical to realizing the full potential of quantum computing in IoT. The future promises not only faster and more efficient data processing but also heightened data security and the development of groundbreaking IoT applications across various industries.

D. Predictions for the IoT Industry: Unveiling the Future

The Internet of Things (IoT) has been evolving at a rapid pace, transforming industries, businesses, and everyday life. As IoT technology continues to mature, it's important to look ahead and anticipate the trends that will shape its future. In this exploration, we present predictions for the IoT industry, offering insights into what lies ahead in terms of technological advancements, market trends, and societal impacts.

1. **5G and IoT Integration:** The rollout of 5G networks will accelerate the adoption of IoT devices and applications. With lower latency and higher bandwidth, 5G will enable real-time data transmission, making IoT even more responsive and effective.

2. **Edge Computing Dominance:** Edge computing will become the norm for IoT deployments. Processing data closer to the source, edge computing reduces latency and enhances privacy, making it ideal for critical applications like autonomous vehicles and healthcare.

3. **AI and IoT Convergence:** The integration of artificial intelligence (AI) and IoT will become increasingly prevalent. AI algorithms will be used to analyze the massive amounts of data generated by IoT devices, unlocking valuable insights and enabling predictive analytics.

4. **IoT in Healthcare Boom:** IoT will revolutionize healthcare, leading to the widespread adoption of remote patient monitoring, wearable devices, and telemedicine. This trend will improve patient care and reduce healthcare costs.

5. **Sustainable IoT:** The IoT industry will focus on sustainability, developing energy-efficient devices and promoting eco-friendly practices. Sustainable IoT will contribute to

environmental goals and reduce the industry's carbon footprint.

6. **Blockchain for IoT Security:** To address IoT security concerns, blockchain technology will be integrated into IoT ecosystems. Blockchain's decentralized and tamper-resistant nature will enhance the security and trustworthiness of IoT data.

7. **IoT in Agriculture:** The agriculture sector will increasingly rely on IoT for precision farming, crop monitoring, and livestock management. IoT-enabled agriculture will optimize resource usage and improve food production.

8. **IoT in Smart Cities:** Smart city initiatives will expand, with IoT playing a central role in urban planning, traffic management, waste disposal, and environmental monitoring. This will lead to more efficient and sustainable urban living.

9. **IoT in Industry 4.0:** IoT will continue to drive Industry 4.0, transforming manufacturing processes with automation, predictive maintenance, and real-time monitoring. This will improve productivity and reduce downtime.

10. **Privacy and Regulation:** As IoT data collection grows, privacy concerns will intensify. Stricter regulations and standards for data protection and privacy will emerge, impacting IoT deployments and data usage.

11. **IoT in Education:** IoT will find applications in education,

enhancing the learning experience through smart classrooms, personalized learning, and remote education tools.

12. **Quantum IoT:** Quantum computing will advance IoT capabilities, enabling complex simulations, faster data processing, and more secure encryption methods.

13. **IoT in Space:** IoT will extend its reach to space exploration, with IoT devices on satellites and space probes providing real-time data from the cosmos.

14. **Human Augmentation:** IoT-enabled wearable devices will increasingly merge with human biology, offering health monitoring, augmented reality, and cognitive enhancements.

15. **Ethical AI and IoT:** Ethical considerations in AI and IoT will gain prominence, emphasizing responsible data use, transparency, and fairness.

As the IoT industry continues to evolve, these predictions provide a glimpse into the transformative potential of IoT technology. Embracing these trends and addressing the associated challenges will be key to harnessing the full capabilities of IoT for the benefit of society, businesses, and individuals.

CHAPTER 13

Case Studies and Success Stories

In the world of technology and innovation, nothing speaks louder than real-world results. Case studies and success stories are the living proof of the transformative potential of the Internet of Things (IoT). In this section, we dive into concrete examples and compelling narratives that showcase how IoT is making a tangible impact across various industries and applications. These stories serve as a testament to the power of IoT solutions in solving complex challenges, enhancing efficiency, and driving meaningful change. From smart cities and healthcare to agriculture and industry, these real-life scenarios highlight the IoT's ability to turn vision into reality.

A. Real-world IoT Implementations: Turning Vision into Reality

The Internet of Things (IoT) has evolved from a concept into a reality, with a myriad of real-world implementations spanning industries, businesses, and everyday life. These IoT applications showcase the tangible benefits of connecting devices, gathering data, and making informed decisions. In this exploration, we delve into a range of real-world IoT implementations, highlighting their significance, key components, advantages, and the impact they have on the way we live, work, and interact with the world.

1. **Smart Cities:** The deployment of IoT sensors and systems in smart cities is transforming urban living. Examples include:

- **Traffic Management:** IoT-enabled traffic lights and sensors optimize traffic flow, reducing congestion and emissions.

- **Waste Management:** Smart bins equipped with sensors alert waste collection services when they are full, improving efficiency.

- **Environmental Monitoring:** IoT devices measure air quality, noise levels, and weather conditions to enhance urban sustainability.

2. **Industrial IoT (IIoT):** In the industrial sector, IoT is revolutionizing manufacturing and processes:

- **Predictive Maintenance:** IoT sensors on machinery collect data to predict maintenance needs, reducing downtime and costs.

- **Supply Chain Optimization:** IoT tracking systems improve inventory management and logistics, enhancing efficiency.

- **Quality Control:** IoT sensors monitor product quality in real-time, ensuring consistency.

3. **Healthcare:** IoT is reshaping healthcare by enabling remote monitoring and personalized care:

- **Remote Patient Monitoring:** Wearable IoT devices track vital signs and chronic conditions, allowing for real-time health monitoring.

- **Telemedicine:** IoT facilitates virtual doctor-patient consultations, enhancing access to healthcare services.

- **Medication Adherence:** IoT-enabled pill dispensers remind patients to take their medication, improving adherence.

4. **Agriculture:** IoT has found its place in agriculture, leading to precision farming:

- **Crop Monitoring:** IoT sensors collect data on soil conditions, moisture levels, and crop health for optimized irrigation and fertilization.

- **Livestock Management:** IoT trackers monitor the health and location of livestock, ensuring their well-being.

- **Weather Forecasting:** IoT weather stations provide accurate data for farmers to make informed decisions.

5. **Consumer IoT:** In homes and daily life, IoT devices are becoming commonplace:

- **Smart Homes:** IoT-enabled thermostats, security systems, and appliances offer convenience and energy savings.

- **Wearable Tech:** Smartwatches and fitness trackers collect health data, promoting wellness and fitness.

- **Voice Assistants:** IoT voice-controlled devices like Amazon Echo and Google Home provide hands-free assistance.

6. **Energy and Utilities:** IoT is optimizing energy usage and utility management:

- **Smart Grids:** IoT sensors monitor electricity grids, reducing power outages and improving grid stability.

- **Water Management:** IoT solutions help detect leaks, optimize water usage, and improve water quality.

- **Oil and Gas:** In the energy sector, IoT sensors enhance safety and efficiency in exploration and production.

7. **Environmental Monitoring:** IoT contributes to environmental conservation:

- **Wildlife Tracking:** IoT-enabled collars and tags track animal movements and behavior for conservation efforts.

- **Water Quality:** IoT sensors monitor water bodies for pollution and aquatic life preservation.

- **Climate Change Research:** IoT devices collect climate data for research on global warming and climate patterns.

8. **Retail:** IoT enhances the retail experience:

- **Inventory Management:** RFID tags and IoT sensors provide real-time inventory tracking, reducing stockouts.

- **Customer Insights:** IoT systems analyze customer behavior to improve marketing and store layouts.

- **Checkout-less Stores:** IoT enables cashier-less shopping experiences, like Amazon Go.

These real-world IoT implementations are just the tip of the iceberg, showcasing the transformative potential of IoT across diverse sectors. As technology continues to evolve and IoT solutions become more sophisticated, we can expect even greater innovations and positive impacts on society, businesses, and individuals in the years to come.

B. Industry-specific Use Cases: Tailoring IoT Solutions for Success

The Internet of Things (IoT) is not a one-size-fits-all concept; rather, it's a versatile technology that can be customized to address specific industry needs and challenges. Industry-specific IoT use cases are the exemplars of this adaptability, demonstrating how IoT solutions are tailored to meet the unique requirements of various sectors. In this exploration, we dive into specific industry domains, unveiling how IoT is revolutionizing processes, enhancing efficiency, and driving innovation.

1. Manufacturing (IIoT):

- **Predictive Maintenance:** IoT sensors monitor machinery in real-time, predicting maintenance needs and reducing downtime.

- **Quality Control:** IoT cameras and sensors ensure product quality through automated inspections and defect detection.

- **Supply Chain Visibility:** IoT tracking systems provide end-to-end visibility into the supply chain, optimizing logistics and inventory management.

2. Healthcare:

- **Remote Patient Monitoring:** Wearable IoT devices track vital signs and chronic conditions, enabling continuous care and early intervention.

- **Smart Hospitals:** IoT solutions enhance patient experience through real-time location tracking, bed management, and equipment monitoring.

- **Medication Adherence:** IoT-enabled pill dispensers and medication packaging improve patient compliance.

3. Agriculture (AgTech):

- **Precision Farming:** IoT sensors collect data on soil conditions, moisture levels, and crop health, optimizing irrigation and fertilization.

- **Livestock Monitoring:** IoT trackers ensure the well-being of livestock by tracking their health and location.

- **Climate Control:** IoT weather stations provide accurate data for agricultural decision-making.

4. Retail:

- **Inventory Management:** RFID tags and IoT sensors offer real-time inventory tracking, reducing stockouts and overstocking.

- **Customer Insights:** IoT systems analyze customer behavior to enhance marketing strategies and store layouts.

- **Checkout-less Stores:** IoT enables cashier-less shopping experiences, improving the shopping process.

5. Energy and Utilities:

- **Smart Grids:** IoT sensors monitor electricity grids, reducing power outages and optimizing energy distribution.

- **Water Management:** IoT solutions detect leaks, optimize water usage, and improve water quality.

- **Oil and Gas:** IoT enhances safety and efficiency in exploration, production, and pipeline management.

6. Smart Cities:

- **Traffic Management:** IoT-enabled traffic lights and sensors optimize traffic flow, reducing congestion and emissions.

- **Waste Management:** Smart bins equipped with sensors enhance waste collection efficiency.

- **Environmental Monitoring:** IoT devices measure air quality, noise levels, and weather conditions, promoting urban sustainability.

7. Logistics and Transportation:

- **Fleet Management:** IoT trackers monitor vehicle locations, driver behavior, and maintenance needs.

- **Cold Chain Management:** IoT sensors maintain the integrity of perishable goods during transit.

- **Public Transportation:** IoT enhances passenger experience with real-time schedules and smart ticketing.

8. Finance (FinTech):

- **Asset Tracking:** IoT enables real-time tracking of high-value assets, reducing theft and improving security.

- **ATM Management:** IoT systems monitor ATM health and cash levels, optimizing maintenance and cash replenishment.

- **Smart Payments:** IoT facilitates contactless payments and fraud detection.

9. Environmental Conservation:

- **Wildlife Tracking:** IoT-enabled collars and tags track animal movements and behavior for conservation efforts.

- **Water Quality:** IoT sensors monitor water bodies for pollution and aquatic life preservation.

- **Climate Change Research:** IoT devices collect climate data for research on global warming and climate patterns.

10. Education (EdTech):

- **Smart Classrooms:** IoT solutions enhance learning environments with interactive displays, personalized content, and attendance tracking.

- **Student Safety:** IoT systems ensure student safety through location tracking and emergency alerts.

- **Campus Management:** IoT-enabled infrastructure optimizes resource allocation and energy usage.

Nikhilesh Misha

These industry-specific use cases demonstrate that IoT's adaptability knows no bounds. By tailoring IoT solutions to meet sector-specific demands, organizations can unlock greater efficiency, innovation, and competitiveness, paving the way for a brighter future in a variety of domains.

C. Challenges and Solutions in IoT Implementation

The implementation of Internet of Things (IoT) solutions brings tremendous opportunities for efficiency, innovation, and data-driven decision-making across various industries. However, it also comes with its fair share of challenges. In this exploration, we delve into the key challenges faced during IoT implementation and propose solutions to address them.

1. Security and Privacy:

- **Challenge:** IoT devices can be vulnerable to cyberattacks, posing risks to data integrity, privacy, and even public safety.

- **Solution:** Implement robust security measures, including encryption, authentication, and regular software updates. Regularly assess and update security protocols to stay ahead of evolving threats.

2. Interoperability:

- **Challenge:** IoT ecosystems often comprise devices from different manufacturers with varying communication protocols, making interoperability a challenge.

- **Solution:** Adopt open standards and protocols to ensure compatibility among devices. Use middleware and gateways to bridge communication between devices with different protocols.

3. Data Management:

- **Challenge:** IoT generates massive amounts of data, requiring efficient storage, processing, and analytics capabilities.

- **Solution:** Leverage cloud computing and edge computing for data storage and processing. Implement data compression techniques to reduce storage requirements. Use advanced analytics and machine learning for actionable insights.

4. Scalability:

- **Challenge:** Expanding an IoT network to accommodate a growing number of devices and users can be complex and costly.

- **Solution:** Design the architecture with scalability in mind. Use cloud-based platforms that can easily accommodate additional devices and users. Implement load balancing to distribute workloads efficiently.

5. Energy Efficiency:

- **Challenge:** Many IoT devices are battery-powered, requiring efficient energy management to extend their lifespan.

- **Solution:** Optimize device firmware to minimize power consumption during idle periods. Utilize low-power communication protocols like NB-IoT or LoRaWAN. Consider energy harvesting solutions like solar panels or kinetic energy.

6. Regulatory Compliance:

- **Challenge:** IoT deployments must adhere to various industry-specific regulations, such as healthcare (HIPAA) or data protection (GDPR).

- **Solution:** Stay informed about relevant regulations and standards in your industry. Implement compliance measures such as data encryption, consent management, and data access controls.

7. Cost Management:

- **Challenge:** The initial cost of IoT deployment, including hardware, software, and infrastructure, can be substantial.

- **Solution:** Conduct a cost-benefit analysis to determine the ROI of IoT implementation. Consider scalability and long-term savings in operational costs.

8. Data Privacy Concerns:

- **Challenge:** Collecting and analyzing personal data through IoT devices raises privacy concerns and may lead to legal challenges.

- **Solution:** Implement strong data anonymization and consent management practices. Clearly communicate data collection and usage policies to users.

9. Legacy System Integration:

- **Challenge:** Integrating IoT with existing legacy systems can be complex and may require retrofitting or replacement.

- **Solution:** Choose IoT solutions with compatibility in mind. Use gateways and middleware to bridge the gap between IoT devices and legacy systems.

10. Ethical Considerations:

- **Challenge:** IoT applications may raise ethical concerns regarding surveillance, data ownership, and the impact on employment.

- **Solution:** Address ethical concerns through transparent communication, ethical frameworks, and responsible data use policies.

Addressing these challenges proactively and strategically is essential for the successful implementation of IoT solutions. By doing so, organizations can unlock the full potential of IoT technology while mitigating risks and ensuring the security, privacy, and scalability of their deployments.

Conclusion

As we draw the final curtain on this journey through these pages, we invite you to reflect on the knowledge, insights, and discoveries that have unfolded before you. Our exploration of various subjects has been a captivating voyage into the depths of understanding.

In these chapters, we have ventured through the intricacies of numerous topics and examined the key concepts and findings that define these fields. It is our hope that you have found inspiration, enlightenment, and valuable takeaways that resonate with you on your own quest for knowledge.

Remember that the pursuit of understanding is an ever-evolving journey, and this book is but a milestone along the way. The world of knowledge is vast and boundless, offering endless opportunities for exploration and growth.

As you conclude this book, we encourage you to carry forward the torch of curiosity and continue your exploration of these subjects. Seek out new perspectives, engage in meaningful discussions, and embrace the thrill of lifelong learning.

We express our sincere gratitude for joining us on this intellectual adventure. Your curiosity and dedication to expanding your horizons are the driving forces behind our shared quest for wisdom and insight.

Thank you for entrusting us with a portion of your intellectual journey. May your pursuit of knowledge lead you to new heights and inspire others to embark on their own quests for understanding.

With profound gratitude,

Nikhilesh Mishra, Author

Recap of Key Takeaways

Throughout your journey in "Mastering the Internet of Things (IoT): Concepts, Techniques, and Applications," you've embarked on a comprehensive exploration of the IoT landscape, delving into its core concepts, practical techniques, and diverse applications. As you reach the conclusion of this enlightening odyssey, let's recap some of the key takeaways that will serve as pillars of knowledge and guidance in your IoT endeavors:

1. **Definition and Evolution of IoT:**

   - IoT is the interconnection of physical devices and objects through the internet, enabling them to collect, exchange, and act upon data.

   - IoT has evolved from simple machine-to-machine (M2M) communication to a vast ecosystem of interconnected devices and systems.

2. **Key Concepts (Sensors, Connectivity, Data):**

   - Sensors are the sensory organs of IoT, capturing data from the physical world.

   - Connectivity is the lifeline of IoT, enabling data transmission between devices and the cloud.

   - Data is the currency of IoT, driving insights and

decision-making.

3. **IoT Ecosystem:**

- The IoT ecosystem encompasses devices, networks, data, cloud services, and applications.

- It operates in a cycle of data collection, processing, and action.

4. **Benefits and Challenges:**

- IoT offers benefits such as improved efficiency, enhanced decision-making, and new business models.

- Challenges include security concerns, interoperability issues, and data privacy considerations.

5. **IoT Hardware:**

- IoT hardware includes sensors, actuators, microcontrollers, communication protocols, power management, and edge computing devices.

6. **IoT Connectivity:**

- Wired and wireless communication technologies play a vital role in IoT connectivity.

- IoT networking technologies like 5G, NB-IoT, and Zigbee provide diverse options for device communication.

7. **IoT Data Management:**

- Data collection, storage, processing, and analytics are crucial for deriving value from IoT.

- Real-time and batch processing techniques cater to different IoT use cases.

8. **IoT Platforms and Middleware:**

- IoT platforms and middleware facilitate device management, data integration, and application development.

- Integration with enterprise systems ensures IoT solutions align with organizational goals.

9. **IoT Application Development:**

- Programming languages, application frameworks, testing, and continuous integration are essential for IoT application development.

10. **IoT Security:**

- Security in IoT devices, secure communication, data encryption, and authentication are paramount.

- Following security best practices and adhering to

standards and regulations are crucial.

11. IoT Protocols:

- MQTT, CoAP, HTTP, and DDS are important IoT protocols, each suited to specific use cases.

- Interoperability between devices and systems is facilitated by standardized protocols.

12. IoT Use Cases and Applications:

- IoT has a wide range of applications, including Smart Cities, Industrial IoT (IIoT), healthcare, agriculture, consumer IoT, automotive, and energy and utilities.

13. Edge and Fog Computing in IoT:

- Edge computing brings processing closer to IoT devices for real-time decision-making.

- Fog computing extends this concept, enabling more complex processing at the network's edge.

14. Advanced IoT Topics:

- Emerging trends like blockchain, quantum computing, AI, IoT in space, and ethical IoT present exciting opportunities and challenges.

15. **Future Trends in IoT:**

- Edge AI, IoT in healthcare, quantum computing's impact, and predictions for the IoT industry shape the future of IoT.

These key takeaways serve as a foundation for your continued exploration and mastery of the Internet of Things. As you move forward, remember that IoT is a dynamic field, constantly evolving with new technologies and innovations. Stay curious, adapt to change, and continue to push the boundaries of what's possible in the world of IoT. Your journey has only just begun.

The Future of IoT

As you conclude your exploration of "Mastering the Internet of Things (IoT): Concepts, Techniques, and Applications," it's essential to peer into the crystal ball of the future and consider how the Internet of Things (IoT) will continue to evolve and shape the world in the years to come. The future of IoT is a landscape defined by innovation, transformation, and the ongoing quest for efficiency, connectivity, and sustainability.

1. **Edge AI and IoT:**

    -   Edge AI, the convergence of artificial intelligence (AI) and IoT at the edge of networks, is poised to become a dominant trend.

    -   Devices and sensors will increasingly process data locally, enabling real-time decision-making without relying solely on cloud services.

    -   Edge AI will drive efficiency and reduce latency, making IoT applications even more responsive and capable.

2. **IoT in Healthcare Revolution:**

    -   The healthcare industry will undergo a substantial IoT-driven transformation.

- Remote patient monitoring, wearable health devices, and smart healthcare facilities will revolutionize patient care, reduce costs, and enhance the quality of healthcare services.

3. **Quantum Computing and IoT Impact:**

   - As quantum computing matures, it will significantly impact IoT.

   - Quantum computing can solve complex problems and optimize algorithms, enhancing data analytics and security for IoT applications.

4. **Predictions for IoT Industry:**

   - IoT adoption will continue to surge across industries, leading to more innovative applications.

   - Interoperability standards will become even more critical as IoT ecosystems expand.

   - AI and machine learning will be integrated into IoT devices for predictive analytics and automation.

   - IoT will play a pivotal role in advancing smart cities, precision agriculture, and environmental monitoring.

   - Energy-efficient IoT solutions will become a priority as sustainability concerns grow.

5. **Security and Privacy in the Future:**

- As IoT adoption increases, the focus on security and privacy will intensify.

- Robust encryption, improved authentication methods, and advanced security protocols will be essential.

- Regulatory bodies will likely introduce stricter IoT security and data privacy regulations.

6. **5G and IoT Synergy:**

- The rollout of 5G networks will provide IoT with high-speed, low-latency connectivity, enabling new applications and services.

- Smart cities, autonomous vehicles, and industrial automation will benefit from 5G's capabilities.

7. **Blockchain Integration:**

- Blockchain technology will find its way into IoT to enhance data integrity, security, and trust.

- It will be used in supply chain management, device identity verification, and data sharing among IoT devices.

8. **Ethical IoT:**

- Ethical considerations surrounding IoT, such as data ownership, bias in algorithms, and responsible AI use, will become more prominent.

- Ethical guidelines and standards will be established to ensure the responsible deployment of IoT solutions.

The future of IoT is a landscape rich with opportunities for innovation, improved quality of life, and environmental sustainability. As IoT technologies mature and intertwine with other emerging fields like AI, quantum computing, and blockchain, they will continue to push the boundaries of what's possible. It is a future where connected devices not only enhance convenience and efficiency but also contribute to addressing some of the world's most pressing challenges. As a master of IoT concepts and techniques, you are well-positioned to be a catalyst for these transformative changes and to shape the future of this dynamic field. Your journey in IoT has the potential to make a profound impact on industries, communities, and the world at large. Embrace the opportunities, stay curious, and keep innovating as you venture into the future of IoT.

Glossary of Terms

The Internet of Things (IoT) is a complex and evolving field with its own set of terminology and jargon. To help you navigate the IoT landscape more effectively, here is a glossary of key terms and concepts you've encountered in "Mastering the Internet of Things (IoT): Concepts, Techniques, and Applications":

1.   **IoT (Internet of Things):** A network of interconnected physical objects or "things" that communicate and exchange data over the internet, often with minimal human intervention.

2.   **Sensors:** Devices that detect and measure physical parameters such as temperature, humidity, light, motion, and more. They are a fundamental component of IoT.

3.   **Actuators:** Devices that take actions based on data received from sensors. For example, turning on a fan when the temperature rises.

4.   **Microcontrollers:** Compact computing devices embedded in IoT devices to control their operations and communicate with other devices.

5.   **Communication Protocols:** Standards governing how data is transmitted between IoT devices. Common protocols include Wi-Fi, Bluetooth, LoRa, Zigbee, and cellular networks

like 5G and NB-IoT.

6. **Power Management:** Techniques for optimizing the power consumption of IoT devices to extend their battery life or reduce energy costs.

7. **Edge Computing:** Processing data closer to the source (at the edge of the network) to reduce latency and improve real-time decision-making.

8. **Wired and Wireless Communication:** Methods of transmitting data within IoT systems, including Ethernet, Wi-Fi, and cellular communication.

9. **IoT Networking Technologies:** Specialized technologies designed for IoT communication, such as Zigbee, Z-Wave, and Thread.

10. **IoT Device Management:** The process of provisioning, monitoring, and maintaining IoT devices over their lifecycle.

11. **Data Collection:** The process of gathering data from sensors and other sources in IoT devices.

12. **Data Storage:** Methods for storing IoT data, including cloud, edge, and fog computing.

13. **Data Processing and Analytics:** Techniques for

analyzing IoT data to extract valuable insights and make informed decisions.

14. **Real-time and Batch Processing:** Methods for handling data processing tasks in real-time or in scheduled batches.

15. **Data Privacy:** Measures and regulations that protect the confidentiality of IoT data and the privacy of individuals.

16. **IoT Platforms:** Software frameworks that provide tools for developing, managing, and analyzing IoT applications.

17. **Middleware:** Software that acts as an intermediary between IoT devices and applications, facilitating communication and data processing.

18. **IoT Device Management Platforms:** Tools and services for remotely managing and maintaining large fleets of IoT devices.

19. **Integration with Enterprise Systems:** Connecting IoT data and processes with existing enterprise software and systems.

20. **Programming Languages for IoT:** Languages commonly used for IoT application development, such as Python, C/C++, and JavaScript.

21.   **Security in IoT Devices:** Measures to protect IoT devices from cyberattacks and unauthorized access.

22.   **Secure Communication:** Ensuring that data transmitted between IoT devices and servers is encrypted and protected.

23.   **Data Encryption and Authentication:** Methods for securing data through encryption and verifying device identities.

24.   **Security Best Practices:** Recommended guidelines and strategies to enhance IoT security.

25.   **IoT Security Standards and Regulations:** Industry-specific and government-mandated security standards and compliance requirements.

26.   **IoT Protocols:** Communication protocols designed for IoT, including MQTT, CoAP, HTTP, and DDS.

27.   **IoT Interoperability:** Ensuring that different IoT devices and systems can communicate and work together seamlessly.

28.   **Smart Cities:** Urban environments that use IoT technologies to enhance infrastructure, transportation, and services.

29.   **Industrial IoT (IIoT):** The application of IoT in

industrial settings to improve efficiency, maintenance, and production.

30. **Healthcare and Wearables:** IoT applications in healthcare, including wearable devices for monitoring health.

31. **Agriculture and Environmental Monitoring:** IoT solutions for precision agriculture and environmental data collection.

32. **Consumer IoT:** IoT devices and applications for personal use, such as smart homes and wearable technology.

33. **Automotive and Transportation:** IoT's impact on vehicle connectivity, autonomous driving, and transportation logistics.

34. **Energy and Utilities:** IoT's role in optimizing energy consumption, grid management, and utility services.

35. **Edge Computing Architecture:** The structure and components of edge computing systems.

36. **Fog Computing Concepts:** Extending edge computing with fog computing to handle more complex processing tasks.

37. **Edge AI and Machine Learning:** Implementing AI and machine learning algorithms on IoT devices at the edge.

38.   **Real-time Processing at the Edge:** Processing data immediately at the edge to enable rapid decision-making.

39.   **Use Cases for Edge and Fog Computing:** Practical applications of edge and fog computing in various industries.

40.   **Blockchain and IoT:** Integrating blockchain technology to enhance security, trust, and transparency in IoT.

41.   **Quantum Computing and IoT:** The potential impact of quantum computing on IoT data processing and encryption.

42.   **AI and Machine Learning in IoT:** Leveraging AI and ML to extract insights and predictive capabilities from IoT data.

43.   **IoT in Space and Satellite Communication:** IoT applications in space exploration and satellite communication.

44.   **Ethical and Sustainable IoT:** Considering ethical implications and sustainability in IoT design and deployment.

As you continue your journey in IoT, this glossary will serve as a valuable reference for understanding and communicating the intricacies of this dynamic and transformative field. Stay curious, explore new horizons, and use your IoT expertise to shape a more connected and efficient world.

Resources and References

As you reach the final pages of this book by Nikhilesh Mishra, consider it not an ending but a stepping stone. The pursuit of knowledge is an unending journey, and the world of information is boundless.

Discover a World Beyond These Pages

We extend a warm invitation to explore a realm of boundless learning and discovery through our dedicated online platform: **www.nikhileshmishra.com**. Here, you will unearth a carefully curated trove of resources and references to empower your quest for wisdom.

Unleash the Potential of Your Mind

- **Digital Libraries:** Immerse yourself in vast digital libraries, granting access to books, research papers, and academic treasures.

- **Interactive Courses:** Engage with interactive courses and lectures from world-renowned institutions, nurturing your thirst for knowledge.

- **Enlightening Talks:** Be captivated by enlightening talks delivered by visionaries and experts from diverse fields.

- **Community Connections:** Connect with a global community of like-minded seekers, engage in meaningful discussions, and share your knowledge journey.

Your Journey Has Just Begun

Your journey as a seeker of knowledge need not end here. Our website awaits your exploration, offering a gateway to an infinite universe of insights and references tailored to ignite your intellectual curiosity.

Acknowledgments

As I stand at this pivotal juncture, reflecting upon the completion of this monumental work, I am overwhelmed with profound gratitude for the exceptional individuals who have been instrumental in shaping this remarkable journey.

In Loving Memory

To my father, **Late Shri Krishna Gopal Mishra,** whose legacy of wisdom and strength continues to illuminate my path, even in his physical absence, I offer my deepest respect and heartfelt appreciation.

The Pillars of Support

My mother**, Mrs. Vijay Kanti Mishra,** embodies unwavering resilience and grace. Your steadfast support and unwavering faith in my pursuits have been the bedrock of my journey.

To my beloved wife, **Mrs. Anshika Mishra,** your unshakable belief in my abilities has been an eternal wellspring of motivation. Your constant encouragement has propelled me to reach new heights.

My daughter, **Miss Aarvi Mishra,** infuses my life with boundless joy and unbridled inspiration. Your insatiable curiosity serves as a constant reminder of the limitless power of exploration and discovery.

Brothers in Arms

To my younger brothers, **Mr. Ashutosh Mishra** and **Mr. Devashish Mishra,** who have steadfastly stood by my side, offering unwavering support and shared experiences that underscore the strength of familial bonds.

A Journey Shared

This book is a testament to the countless hours of dedication and effort that have gone into its creation. I am immensely grateful for the privilege of sharing my knowledge and insights with a global audience.

Readers, My Companions

To all the readers who embark on this intellectual journey alongside me, your curiosity and unquenchable thirst for knowledge inspire me to continually push the boundaries of understanding in the realm of cloud computing.

With profound appreciation and sincere gratitude,

Nikhilesh Mishra

September 08, 2023

About the Author

Nikhilesh Mishra is an extraordinary visionary, propelled by an insatiable curiosity and an unyielding passion for innovation. With a relentless commitment to exploring the boundaries of knowledge and technology, Nikhilesh has embarked on an exceptional journey to unravel the intricate complexities of our world.

Hailing from the vibrant and diverse landscape of India, Nikhilesh's pursuit of knowledge has driven him to plunge deep into the world of discovery and understanding from a remarkably young age. His unwavering determination and quest for innovation have not only cemented his position as a thought leader but have also earned him global recognition in the ever-evolving realm of technology and human understanding.

Over the years, Nikhilesh has not only mastered the art of translating complex concepts into accessible insights but has also crafted a unique talent for inspiring others to explore the limitless possibilities of human potential.

Nikhilesh's journey transcends the mere boundaries of expertise; it is a transformative odyssey that challenges conventional wisdom and redefines the essence of exploration. His commitment to pushing the boundaries and reimagining the norm serves as a luminous beacon of inspiration to all those who aspire to make a profound impact in the world of knowledge.

As you navigate the intricate corridors of human understanding and innovation, you will not only gain insight into Nikhilesh's expertise but also experience his unwavering dedication to empowering readers like you. Prepare to be enthralled as he seamlessly melds intricate insights with real-world applications, igniting the flames of curiosity and innovation within each reader.

Nikhilesh Mishra's work extends beyond the realm of authorship; it is a reflection of his steadfast commitment to shaping the future of knowledge and exploration. It is an embodiment of his boundless dedication to disseminating wisdom for the betterment of individuals worldwide.

Prepare to be inspired, enlightened, and empowered as you embark on this transformative journey alongside Nikhilesh Mishra. Your understanding of the world will be forever enriched, and your passion for exploration and innovation will reach new heights under his expert guidance.

Sincerely, **A Fellow Explorer**

Notes

Notes

Notes

Notes

Notes

Notes

Notes

Notes

Notes

Notes

Notes

Notes

www.ingramcontent.com/pod-product-compliance
Lightning Source LLC
LaVergne TN
LVHW051429050326
832903LV00030BD/2995